Psychology in Sheffield: The Early Years

Psychology in Sheffield:
The Early Years

Peter Warr

Institute of Work Psychology
University of Sheffield
United Kingdom

Sheffield
Academic Press

www.SheffieldAcademicPress.com

Published by Sheffield Academic Press Ltd
Mansion House
19 Kingfield Road
Sheffield S11 9AS
England
www.SheffieldAcademicPress.com

Typeset by the Department of Psychology
University of Sheffield
and
printed in the UK

British Library Cataloguing in Publication Data

A catalogue record for this book is available from the British Library

ISBN 1 84127 272 8

CONTENTS

PREFACE

In the first half of the last century it was usual for students of psychology to be examined about the history of their subject, being required to evaluate and compare the main themes developed by principal psychologists of the past. It was widely believed that an appreciation of present work depended upon an understanding of earlier ideas and investigations. "A psychological sophistication that contains no component of historical orientation seems to me to be no sophistication at all" (Boring, 1929, 1950, p. ix). (See also Esper, 1964; Flugel, 1933, 1951, 1964; Hearnshaw, 1964; Murphy, 1928, 1929, 1932, 1938, 1949.)

This interest in psychology's past diminished in later years, for several reasons. As the empirical knowledge base became ever larger, new and expanded courses squeezed the study of history out of a congested academic timetable. Greater specialization into separate sub-divisions led many psychologists to become interested in only a part of the overall subject. University staff were typically selected and promoted for their expertise in methodological, statistical or computer techniques, and a concern for historical or philosophical issues was viewed as of limited career importance.

This expansion, specialization and technique-orientation made it less likely that historical developments would be studied in the manner that was appropriate for earlier years. Furthermore, enlargement of the profession was primarily through substantial recruitment of younger psychologists; younger people are less likely to think in historical terms than are their older colleagues.

However, the tide of interest has begun to turn. Associated with the centenary of the American Psychological Association and the British Psychological Society in 1992 and 2001 respectively, and the half-centenaries of several European societies around the present time, historical accounts and interpretations are becoming more common. The volume edited by Bunn, Lovie and Richards (2001) is described as 'a celebration of British psychology over the last century'.

The present book has a more restricted focus: the development of psychology in the University of Sheffield between 1906 and 1970. The goal is to provide information that can be used in relation to other academic departments and in building up overall accounts of British psychology across the period. Sheffield was both typical of the national pattern and distinctive in that its achievements were among the best.

I am very grateful to the many people who have contributed to the preparation of this book. Information was kindly provided by most psychologists in Sheffield between 1955 and 1970, both about themselves and about others whose location was initially unknown to me. This information has been invaluable throughout the chapters that follow, and in the summaries about each person that are collated in Appendix 1.

Particular thanks are due to Harry Kay, who made available a considerable number of important documents from the 1960s and whose detailed recollections were of immense help. Harry also assisted by commenting on a draft of part of the material, as did several other members of staff from that period. Among those, Kevin Connolly contributed particular assistance through discussions and links with previous members of the department. Len Hetherington worked wonders on photographs from the 1960s and earlier.

I learned about several developments only through examination of documents held in different parts of the University of Sheffield. I am grateful to Lawrence Aspden, Nigel Dandy, Ann James and other colleagues for their considerable help in locating original material.

I am also indebted to members of other psychology departments for information about their own local history, and to Elizabeth Valentine, of Royal Holloway, University of London, for encouragement and ideas. I hope that others will be able to prepare similar accounts of the early years of psychology in their own universities.

Some obstacles to historical research are financial. Becoming immersed in a period and its people requires considerable time, and publication of a historical account is expensive. The University of Sheffield has been generous in its provision of both opportunities for research and funds for publication.

This examination of one university may serve as a building-block in the construction of comprehensive histories of British psychology. It is written with that in mind, and also in the hope that readers will find parts of its content of personal interest to them.

Peter Warr
February 2001

1. THE FIRST HALF-CENTURY:
EDUCATION, MEDICINE AND PHILOSOPHY

A Psychology Department was formally established in the University of Sheffield on 1 January 1960. However, aspects of the subject had been taught in courses of education and medicine during the previous five decades.

The progress of psychology in Sheffield during that earlier period was similar to developments in the country more widely. A separate scientific discipline of psychology, with formal teaching and specialist periodicals, had begun to emerge around the turn of the century, and the Psychological Society was created in 1901 (becoming the British Psychological Society in 1906) (Edgell, 1947). However, progress was slow before the second world war, with the total lecturing staff in British departments of psychology in 1939 numbering only about thirty (Hearnshaw, 1964, p. 208)[1]. Advances in Britain were much less marked than in some other countries, notably the United States of America and Germany (Boring, 1950).

Hearnshaw (1962, p. 6) suggests that "the main responsibility for this relative backsliding must be placed . . . . on our very conservative universities. . . . . [I]n the organization and public support of science until well into the present century [Britain] lagged far behind other Western countries. . . . . It is hardly surprising that universities which had only just become aware of the need to provide laboratories for teaching and research in the physical and biological sciences should not have regarded the establishment of psychological laboratories as a very urgent requirement". In practice, any competition for laboratory resources would have been with other scientific departments, and there was disagreement early in the century about how far psychology should be viewed as empirically scientific in the manner of traditional sciences.

It was usual for the subject to be seen as falling within Arts rather than Science faculties. In those faculties, scepticism or overt hostility from established philosophers was widespread early in the century. There was extended debate about the proper object (if there was one) of psychological study and about possible methods of inquiry. "It was, we may surmise, the doubts and inhibitions engendered by this long philosophical debate during the first half of the twentieth century which

---

[1] However, in some universities psychology was also taught in other departments.

1

retarded the development of British psychology and blocked its academic growth. For unenthusiastic philosophers were in a key position to advise on matters still generally regarded as falling within their key province" (Hearnshaw, 1964, p. 211).

The restraining power of philosophers was seen particularly clearly in the University of Oxford, where undergraduate psychology teaching was not introduced until 1947. Morrell (1997, p. 92) suggests that the Oxford philosophers' "attitude to psychologists was generally like lions looking for prey: with their well-groomed conservatism they objected to behaviouristic animal and comparative psychology, suspected the claims made by psychotherapists . . . , and deemed experimental psychology to be dangerous and fraudulent".

More broadly, economic circumstances in the 1920s and 1930s (the 'great depression') severely restricted the expansion of universities. Even within established disciplines, resources were extremely limited, so that the development of new subjects such as psychology was inevitably given low priority. Academic departments, especially in Arts faculties, were tiny, and staff naturally focussed on their own core concerns.

Limited and sometimes intermittent psychological developments occurred in the Universities of Aberdeen, Bristol (to 1920), Cambridge, Edinburgh, Glasgow, Liverpool (to 1914), London (Bedford, Kings and University Colleges), Manchester, Oxford, Reading and St Andrews (Flugel, 1954; Hearnshaw, 1964; Knight, 1962; Morrell, 1997; Oldfield, 1950; Pear, 1955; Valentine, 1997, 1998, 1999; Wooldridge, 1994). However, "in the majority of British universities before 1945 there was no provision, or only the slenderest provision, for teaching and research in psychology" (Hearnshaw, 1962, p. 7).

Nevertheless, academic psychological work was taking place. "Psychology was saved by its applications, educational, industrial and medical. Here indubitably, and beyond the boundaries of philosophic controversy, progress was being made . . . . . Psychologists were needed, and the universities had to train them. It was this more than anything else that surmounted the obstructiveness of philosophic sceptics" (Hearnshaw, 1964, p. 211). Wooldridge (1994) makes the same point in this way: "The development of English psychology before the second world war was highly eccentric: impoverished as a branch of pure research but innovative as an applied discipline" (p. 56).

The importance of educational, industrial and medical psychology had been dramatised in 1919, when a small, introverted British Psychological Society was warned that alternative groups were about to be established to act on behalf of those three applied areas. In order to avoid loss of potential members, substantial changes to the Society were introduced in a very short time, creating specialised sections for each sub-domain over and above the previous single, rather academic focus (Lovie, 1998).

Of those three applied areas, industrial psychology in the United Kingdom was restricted to a very small number of centres. In London, the Industrial Fatigue Research Board was established by the Department of Scientific and Industrial Research and the Medical Research Council in 1918. This was renamed the Industrial Health Research Board in 1927, and continued in limited operation until 1959 (Shimmin and Wallis, 1994; Warr, 1999). The Board also supported a few researchers in the 1930s at the University of Cambridge (e.g., Dr E. G. Chambers, Dr E. Farmer, Dr A. Heim), at the University of Manchester (e.g., Dr S. Wyatt) and the London School of Tropical Medicine (Dr T. Bedford). Its influence was limited, primarily because work was published through relatively inaccessible government documents.

Also in London was the National Institute of Industrial Psychology (NIIP), founded in 1921, with Dr C. S. Myers as Director (following a period at Cambridge University and in war-time applications) (Myers, 1936). That organisation was hampered by a lack of funds, and worked primarily on practical issues of immediate concern to individual companies; its impact on academic departments was thus modest (Shimmin and Wallis, 1994)[2].

At certain periods before the second world war, industrial psychology (later referred to as 'occupational', 'work' or 'industrial and organizational' psychology) was taught at the Universities of Glasgow and Manchester (Shimmin and Wallis, 1994). However, in the pre-war period there appear to have been no industrial psychological activities in the University of Sheffield. Consistent with the general trend, early psychology in Sheffield was focussed on educational and medical applications.

Psychology and the Department of Education

Sheffield University's first psychologist was active almost a century ago. In 1906, John Alfred Green was appointed as the University's first Professor of Education[3]. He had been born in

---

[2] Incidentally, Leslie Hearnshaw, whose broad-ranging historical accounts have been cited above, was on the staff of the NIIP between 1933 and 1938.

[3] The University had been established in the preceding year (1905), although a

Sheffield in 1867, attended school and (as a pupil teacher) evening classes in Sheffield, and obtained a BA degree in Education at the University of London. In 1892, he became a Junior Tutor at Borough Road Teachers' Training College, London, before being appointed Lecturer in Education and Master of Method at University College Bangor in 1894. He was promoted to Professor in 1900, before moving to a new chair in Sheffield in 1906. (A photograph is on page 94.)

The university's <u>Calendar</u> for 1906-1907 describes the two sets of lectures (three hours a week each) for first-year Education students as: 1. The elements of psychology with special reference to mental development; 2. Education of the young in Plato's Republic. By 1907-1908, a 20-lecture course on physiological psychology was included. In addition, students undertook not less than 75 hours practical work. 'Special Lecture Courses for Teachers' were also presented on Saturday mornings. Examples from 1906 include 'Teaching of the mother tongue' and 'History of Education: Locke, Rousseau and Pestalozzi'[4].

Professor Green was influential both within the university and on a wider scientific field. Internally, he was active in management and development of the fledgling university. He was of course responsible for teaching educational psychology, and he expanded the Department of Education to five lecturers in addition to himself. Katharine L. Johnston joined him in 1908, and C. Birchenough in 1909. The former left in 1913, and the latter (to become an Inspector of Schools) in 1919. The five Education Lecturers in 1921 were Woutrina A. Bone, E. J. G. Bradford, Etheldreda M. A. King, J. R. Thompson and W. Vickers. During the 1914-1918 war, C. Birchenough served as a Lieutenant in Italy, and for his army service J. R. Thompson was awarded the Military Cross. Temporary Lecturers in Education were appointed in 1915: Mrs C. Birchenough and Mrs J. A. Green.

J. A. Green died in post in 1922. An obituary notice (Anon, 1922, p. 204) described him as follows:

> He by no means conceived that his work was to be confined within the walls of the University. He did a great work on the Education Committee of the city, and was largely responsible for a recent improvement in the primary schools and for the foundation of new secondary schools, providing free secondary education

University College had been in operation since 1897.
[4] By 1915, 74 students attended the Saturday morning lectures.

in Sheffield. He devoted himself unsparingly to the work of the Workers' Educational Association, which has lost in him its best friend. He represented the University on the Teachers' Registration Council. He was Chairman of the Educational Handwork Association[5].

Professor Green had studied on the spot the educational institutions of France, Germany, Sweden and Switzerland, and had lectured in Russia on English Education. He published a book in 1904 on Pestalozzi, and a larger work in 1912 on the same educational reformer. In 1911 he was joint-author of 'A Primer of Teaching Practice'; in 1912 he published an 'Introduction to Psychology'. He edited the 'Journal of Experimental Pedagogy' until his death[6].

Professor Green ensured that the Department of Education (which was in two faculties, Arts and Pure Science) both provided professional training and carried out academic research into educational psychological issues. As part of a general description of the university, he wrote as follows (Green, 1910, pp. 151-2):

> The Department of Education provides professional training for students of the University Training College, and preparation for the University Diploma in Education for teachers in secondary schools. In addition, Saturday morning courses are given to teachers actually engaged in school work. These courses are of two kinds – on the one hand, there are classes for the demonstration and discussion of practical problems of the class room, and on the other hand, courses of lectures and demonstrations on modern methods of research in education. In connection with these courses, organized work is carried out in some of the schools.

---

[5] 'Educational handwork' at the time was concerned with practical lessons in woodwork, drawing, dressmaking, needlework, silverwork, leatherwork, etc.. Handwork activities were in part viewed from a psychological perspective, emphasising links between motor development and cognitive development, and analysing the intellectual value of different forms of imagery (Ballard, 1910).

[6] Additional information about J. A. Green is provided by Thomas (1982).

> The Department is equipped with the apparatus of a
> small pedagogical research laboratory, including a Hipp
> Chronoscope, McDougall's Attention Machine,
> Rauschberg's Association and Memory Apparatus,
> Netschajef's Reaction Time Apparatus, Ebbinghaus
> Memory Apparatus, Jacquet's Sphygmograph, Romer's
> Voice Key, Minnemann's Card Changing Apparatus,
> Wundt's Tachistoscope, Wundt's Control Hammer,
> Kymograph, &c, &c.

As pointed out by Benjamin (2000), "it is the establishment of the laboratory that marks the transition from philosophy to science" (p. 318). J. A. Green was concerned for the systematic empirical study of learners and teachers, and his interest in psychological measurement during the period is evident from the list of apparatus above. No doubt some items had been collected during his European visits.

In the present context, three themes are particularly important: J. A. Green's interest in intelligence and its measurement, his psychological textbook, and his journal editorship. In the first respect, Sheffield work occurred at the same time as initial developments in other countries and Cyril Burt's early investigations (when he was Lecturer in Experimental Psychology at the University of Liverpool, 1907-1912). Professor Green's international contacts influenced his approach. For example, he worked for a year in Germany (Ward, 1922), and he also had a strong interest in Russian psychology. The Sheffield University Department of Education still holds a test imported by him from Russia in 1912, labelled as providing 'psychological profiles according to the system of G. I. Rossolimo'. A lecturer in the department (Katharine Johnson) was sent to Paris to study Binet's methods, and she translated early Binet-Simon scales and applied them in Sheffield schools (Johnston, 1911a, b)[7]. Miss Johnson left the department in 1913, and further Sheffield investigations with the scales were carried out by her replacement as Lecturer, Nina Taylor, after she had received guidance from Simon in Paris (Taylor, 1916)[8].

The Education Department's concern for mental testing reflected a growing national interest in measurements applied to children and,

---

[7] The first Binet-Simon test of intelligence was published in 1905, with a revision in 1908. The initial focus was on identification of those school-children who needed remedial teaching, rather than on the creation of a general measure of cognitive ability.

[8] Miss Taylor left for a school-teaching position in 1917.

later, to adults. From 1914, all local education authorities were required to provide special schools for children classed as mentally defective, and techniques for assessment became essential. These developments were slowed by the first world war and then by general financial restrictions. However, creation in USA of the Army Alpha and Beta tests (administered in a group rather than to a single individual), and increased testing in education and elsewhere, led to a sustained advance through the 1930s (Boring, 1950; Sutherland, 1984; Wooldridge, 1994).

The Sheffield textbook in the area was written by T. Loveday[9] and J. A. Green. Entitled <u>An Introduction to Psychology, More Especially for Teachers</u>, it was published by Oxford University Press in 1912 and reprinted in 1915. The authors described it in their Preface as "a simple introduction to the subject for the use, more especially, of students of education in our training colleges", and emphasised "particularly our indebtedness to Dr Stout"[10]. "The kind of psychology with which we shall be concerned is commonly called Empirical Psychology . . . . .[W]e have to do with desires, emotions, acts of perceiving, thinking, deciding, and other actual mental events and their conditions. Psychology is thus the study of the way in which minds behave" (p. 11). Experimental methods were described and recommended. "It cannot, however, be too frequently insisted on that success in experimental work depends ultimately upon first-hand study of our own minds" (p. 19).

Chapter headings in the book by Loveday and Green included Infancy, Language, Purpose, Feeling, Perception, Imaging, Conception, Memory, Thought and Imagination, and Self and Character. For each chapter, practical exercises in educational settings were suggested. Intelligence and intelligence testing were not covered; the Preface indicates that they might be treated in a later version, but that was not written.

J. A. Green's third important contribution to psychology was editorial work for the <u>Journal of Experimental Pedagogy</u>. He served as

---

[9] Thomas Loveday had been Sheffield University Librarian between 1907 and 1911. He was Lecturer in Philosophy in the University between 1911 and 1914, moving on to the University of Durham and then Armstrong College, Newcastle-upon-Tyne. He became Principal of University College, Southampton, and (in 1921) Vice-Chancellor of the University of Bristol.

[10] The first edition of G. F. Stout's <u>Manual of Psychology</u> was published in 1898, and the book was revised and re-issued up to 1938. It was the most used textbook of psychology in Britain in the first quarter of the century (Edgell, 1947, p. 114; Hearnshaw, 1964, p. 139).

editor of that journal from its inauguration in 1911 until his death in 1922[11]. 'Experimental pedagogy' was a term popular in Germany, France and elsewhere, to describe empirical approaches to the study of learning and teaching. By 1911, a bibliography on the subject published in Paris contained as many as 4,027 items (Wooldridge, 1994, p. 54). The Journal published a substantial number of psychological investigations applicable to education (from authors such as Ballard, Burt, Drever, Lloyd Morgan, Spearman, Thompson, Winch, Wyatt and Valentine), and was superseded in 1923 by the Forum of Education, which became in 1931 the British Journal of Educational Psychology[12].

The Sheffield Department of Education in the first quarter of the century was unusual for its strong emphasis on quantitative, empirical psychology. Research papers covered the psychological bases of school geography (Birchenough, 1911) and empirical comparisons between methods of teaching reading and teaching spelling (Gill, 1912a, b). Miss E. M. A. King[13] contributed statistical expertise and calculations (Green, 1920, p. 246). J. A. Green's own papers in the Journal of Experimental Pedagogy concerned backward children, the teaching of English, the work of Rossollimo, Montessori and Pestalozzi (whose publications he translated and expanded in two books), processes of arithmetical thinking, teacher performance, and the nature of intelligence. In addition, he published a Primer of Teaching Practice (with C. Birchenough in 1914) and contributed many dozens of book reviews. More generally, he was a keen member of the recently formed (1906) British Psychological Society (known as the Psychological Society between 1901 and 1906).

The University's second and third Professors of Education (G. H. Turnbull[14] and W. H. G. (Harry) Armytage) were both trained as historians, so that their contributions were less directly in psychological areas. However, psychology continued to be taught in their department, primarily to teachers or trainee teachers, but also through contributions to General degrees in Education.

---

[11] It was printed in Sheffield by J. W. Northend, 8 Norfolk Row.

[12] The latter two were edited between 1923 and 1955 by psychologist C. W. Valentine, Professor of Education at the University of Birmingham until 1946. Professor Valentine was External Examiner to the Sheffield Department of Education between 1919 and 1921.

[13] Miss King was appointed a Temporary Assistant Lecturer in Education in 1917, and confirmed as a Lecturer in 1919.

[14] G. H. Turnbull took up his post in 1922, having been a Lecturer in Education at the University of Liverpool since 1914. He served as Professor until 1954.

Candidates for the Diploma of Education were required already to have a degree or equivalent qualification; the course lasted one year. For both the Diploma and a General degree in Education, students covered developmental psychology, habit, thinking, imagination, language, personality, experimental procedures, techniques of assessment, and sometimes physiological psychology. In addition, staff in the department were very active (within a general University policy) in providing 'extension courses' and classes for the Workers' Educational Association. Many such courses in psychology and social psychology were given each year by E. J. G. Bradford (to 1952), J. A. Green (to 1922), J. R. Thompson (to 1953) and W. Vickers (to 1929)[15].

Several members of the Department of Education between the 1920s and 1950s published reports of psychological research, typically examining measures of abilities and their psychometric properties. Papers by E. J. G. Bradford included 'Reliability coefficients' (1921, Journal of Experimental Pedagogy), 'The relationship of intelligence to size of family in the different occupational grades' (1937, British Journal of Educational Psychology), 'Short tests of low-grade intelligence' (1940, Occupational Psychology), and 'Selection for technical education' (1945, British Journal of Educational Psychology). (Mr Bradford was active during the 1939-1945 war in psychological testing of service-people.) Examples of J. R. Thompson's publications include 'The interference factor in mental processes: An experiment in correlation and transfer' (1921, Journal of Experimental Pedagogy) and 'Boundary conditions for correlations between three or four variables' (1928, British Journal of Psychology). He received a Doctor of Science degree from Durham University in 1928 for his Correlation and Theory of Mental Ability. W. Vickers published, for instance, 'Results from some new tests of practical abilities' (1928, British Journal of Psychology)[16].

E. J. G. Bradford also published works in aspects of geography, such as The Nature of Europe: A Book for Schools (1928) and The Lands of the American Peoples (1933). His combined psychological

---

[15] Much psychology teaching of these kinds was also provided by Dr David Crowther (in the Department of Extramural Studies between 1928 and 1963) and Dr Bertram Laing (Lecturer in Philosophy to 1945 and Professor of Philosophy from 1945 to 1949).

[16] Mr Vickers left to become a Schools Inspector in 1929. Mr Bradford and Dr Thompson (both appointed in 1920) continued in post until retiring in 1952 and 1953 respectively; they were both promoted to Senior Lecturers in 1946. After retirement, Mr Bradford contributed to a psychological clinic at Middlewood Hospital, and Dr Thompson undertook some part-time teaching in the university.

and geographical interests were illustrated in 'The measurement of perspective in geographical outlook' (1932, <u>British Journal of Educational Psychology</u>). This breadth of activity is linked to the fact that persons practising psychology in the first half of the century reached that position through a variety of different routes. There were no standard degree courses and no professional psychological qualifications, and the title 'psychologist' was open to people of widely varying knowledge and experience. For example, Mr Bradford had been a geography school-teacher before joining the University staff, and he extended his interests in intelligence and performance testing from that base. His psychological publications and contributions to the discipline led to him later being awarded a Fellowship of the British Psychological Society.

Psychology and the Faculty of Medicine

Students of medicine received some instruction from E. J. G. Bradford as a Lecturer in Normal Psychology between 1928 and 1934. It may be that a more medical emphasis was later considered desirable, since in December 1934 the Senate accepted a recommendation from the Faculty of Medicine "with reference to the teaching of Psychology to Medical students: (a) A course consisting of 10-12 lectures, supplemented by clinical instruction in Psychological Clinics, should be given in the summer session of the 4th year; (b) This course should be given by a Medical man; (c) The scheme should be reviewed at the end of 3 years." For this work Dr E. F. Skinner was appointed Lecturer in Psychology in the Faculty of Medicine; in fact, he held this post until his death in 1944[17]. He was replaced by Dr J. Carson, who continued part-time in the role until 1957, when psychology teaching for medical students was taken over by the new Psychological Laboratory (see Chapter 2).

The Medical Faculty's first Lecturer in Mental Diseases (the term used for Psychiatry in university documents until 1956-1957) was Dr W. S. Kay. He left in 1911, being replaced by Dr W. J. N. Vincent, who held the post from 1911 to 1933. Subsequent Lecturers in Mental Diseases (usually honorary and part-time) were Dr F. E. E. Schneider (1934-1940), Dr R. S. Kennedy (1938-1939), Dr F. J. S. Esher (1940-

---

[17] Dr Skinner had been employed as a Tutor in Clinical Medicine between 1914 and 1931. He was a Lecturer in Medicine between 1931 and 1944, having responsibilities noted here as a psychology teacher from 1934. The Annual Report for 1939-1940 indicates that he led discussions on 'the psychology of war' in 33 First Aid Posts in the Sheffield area.

1966) and Dr. F. T. Thorpe (1940-1963). In 1928, Dr W. S. Kay gave £100 for 'an annual medal in mental diseases'.

Of those medical lecturers, Fred Esher (1903-1999) made a particular contribution to psychology in Sheffield. He qualified in Medicine (in 1926), but had a strong interest in psychological issues, linked to friendships with John Carl Flugel and Charles Spearman. He was appointed as Medical Officer in charge of the Sheffield Mental Welfare Service in 1936 (for example, inaugurating the Child Guidance Clinic in Newbould Lane in 1937). He was nationally responsible for training Sergeant testers for the substantial psychometric assessment programme that was conducted during the 1939-1945 war (see the next section). The Northern Branch of the British Psychological Society was created by Fred Esher (in 1933), and he long served as its secretary and organiser. During the late 1940s and the 1950s, he gave many talks in Sheffield on a wide range of psychological topics. Dr Esher retired in 1967, but remained an Emeritus Psychiatrist in the city (see Neve, 1997).

The 1940s and Plans for the Future

The University of Sheffield remained very small in the 1940s. The total number of academic staff in 1942-1943 was only 211, of whom 88 were part-time. Within the Department of Education, Dr J. R. Thompson was diverted part-time into the university's Senior Training Corps, assisting with the provision of infantry training. Miss E. M. A. King worked beyond her planned retirement, since no replacement could be found. More generally, government war-time regulations required that university three-year courses were concentrated into 27 months, teaching being in four terms a year rather than three[18].

The growing importance of psychology in this period was demonstrated in a resolution by the Faculty of Pure Science in February 1945 "that a Department of Psychology be established" in that faculty. This possibility had been raised in the previous year by the Professor of Education, G. H. Turnbull. His Memorandum to the Faculty had stressed vocational objectives: degree courses in psychology were needed by potential psychiatric social workers, vocational guidance officers, welfare workers, and psychologists in local education authorities[19]. "Moreover, a Department of Psychology would be able to

---

[18] In air-raids in December 1940, no university building escaped damage, but there was little interference with teaching.

[19] Consistent with Hearnshaw's (1964) more general account, summarised earlier, Professor Turnbull's proposal was explicitly pragmatic rather than conceptual or

give valuable assistance to other departments in the University, e.g., in the Medical Faculty, to the Department of Education, and to a Department of Social Studies, if such a department were set up". Both General and Honours degrees were envisaged.

Given that the subject-matter of psychology was also of relevance to other faculties, a committee of Senate (chaired by the Vice-Chancellor and including all Deans of Faculties and relevant Professors) was asked to examine the matter. That committee reported to Senate in February 1946, as follows:

> 1. The Committee has reviewed the reasons which influenced the Faculty of Pure Science in its decision to recommend the establishment of a Department of Psychology in that Faculty and has considered the need and demand for instruction in Psychology in the University as a whole. It is the unanimous opinion of the Committee that the subject of Psychology is of such importance as to justify the establishment of a separate Department in the University.
> 2. In the view of the Committee the Department, if established, should be in the Faculties of Arts, Pure Science and Medicine, should provide facilities for experimental work, and should be the focal point for studies in all branches of Psychology in those Faculties.
> 3. It is considered that the Head of the Department should be of professorial rank and that when the Professor has been appointed, a full-time lecturer be also appointed. The Committee supports the continuation of the appointment of a special Lecturer for medical undergraduates and feels that this lecturer could be attached to the Staff of the Department of Psychology.
> 4. Accommodation would be necessary for the Professor and his Staff and for a laboratory.

The report was adopted in full, and confirmed by the University Council in December 1946[20]. After the University's first Chair of Psychology had been advertised, nine applications were received and

---

scientific: psychological training is needed for certain jobs.

[20] Acceptance of the Report was proposed by the Vice-Chancellor and seconded by the Bishop of Sheffield.

referees were consulted. Two candidates were interviewed in June 1947, but neither of those was appointed.

In seeking to make this appointment, Sheffield was in competition with several other universities that also advertised Chairs around this time. There was a general shortage of individuals qualified for new positions in psychology, since teaching had been reduced during the war. Conversely, war-time activities had markedly increased the visibility and perceived value of the discipline. For example, all recruits to the British army undertook three days of assessment, administered by Sergeants trained as testers. The battery included the Raven's Matrices test of general intelligence, a verbal test from the National Institute of Industrial Psychology, the Bennett Mechanical Ability Test, an Arithmetic Test devised by P. E. Vernon, a Clerical Test, and a Morse Aptitude Test. Initial allocation to military roles was based on results from these tests, which were generally well received. The selection of army officers also made much use of psychometric assessment: verbal and non-verbal intelligence tests, word association measures, and the Thematic Apperception Test. Role-playing, group discussion and problem-solving exercises were developed, giving rise later to a three-day assessment process at the War Office Selection Board. This Board gave considerable weight to psychological procedures and interpretations[21].

The situation in universities immediately after the war was illustrated by Kay (1996), in reference to the foundation in 1946 of the Experimental Psychology Group (EPG)[22]:

> From the perspective of 1996, it is hard to appreciate just how few British psychologists were in the academic field before 1940. Hence, when in 1946 some of the leading members of that 'happy few' decided to meet regularly to discuss their research, they thought of themselves in a modest way as a Group rather than a Society. Psychologists had worked in many different areas during the war, yet it was not anticipated that the

---

[21] Much of the material in this paragraph was provided by Reg Edwards (see Chapter 2) during discussions in September 1999.

[22] That small group, founded in 1946, was centred on Cambridge and Oxford Universities, with a goal to advance scientific rather than professional issues (thought by its members to be an excessive concern of the British Psychological Society). The Group became the Experimental Psychology Society in December 1958 (Mollon, 1996).

subject was about to begin one of the most fascinating transformations in the post-war academic era.

After 1946 the numbers of University psychology students and researchers shot up, and a mixed lot we were, many of us having spent up to six years in one wartime job or other. Former army majors and veterans from the Pioneer Corps, naval officers and merchant navy seamen rubbed shoulders with ex-Spitfire pilots, conscientious objectors and members of the Land Army. To one in that first wave of post-war psychologists, the EPG's meetings had an extraordinary appeal, making them the most eagerly awaited scientific meetings I have attended. In a decade when books and British journals were rationed as miserly as food – an order for a copy of R. S. Woodworth's Experimental Psychology (1938 edition) took 18 months to arrive – the Group meetings were oases in a thirsty world.

Single-subject Honours degrees in psychology were extremely rare at that time. Most individuals viewing themselves as psychologists had received training in a variety of other disciplines as well as psychology. Some combined their psychological activities with other roles. For example, E. J. G. Bradford's contributions to both psychology and geography have been described above.

Russell and Summerfield (1956) reported a survey of "persons who received degrees or diplomas in psychology during the years 1949-51"[23]. (No differentiation was made in analyses between a diploma and a degree.) Of those with first degrees or diplomas (rather than postgraduate qualifications), 20% had also studied philosophy, 17% had studied social sciences, and 15% had studied languages. Only 6% had taken no other subject. A high proportion (not specified in the paper) had been awarded Bachelor of Education degrees, combining psychology and education as principal subjects[24]. Previous war service meant that students of the period were older than subsequently; 59% of this sample of psychology students were aged 30 or above.

In summary, British academic psychology up to the 1940s was severely impoverished. "Psychology occupied only a lowly position in

---

[23] In practice, about a quarter of the respondents had qualified earlier in the decade; see Russell and Summerfield, 1956, p. 31.

[24] Seventy per cent of that sample were men. The male percentage among psychology students fell to about 25 in the 1990s (Holdstock, 1998).

the academic pecking order" (Wooldridge, 1994, p. 153). There were few students, and the psychological input to their education varied enormously. No national restrictions were placed on the label 'psychologist', and university teachers of the subject may have had little formal psychological training. Few psychologists had received a PhD at this time. Developments in the University of Sheffield were illustrative of a wider pattern in the country as a whole.

In November 1947 the Sheffield University Committee on the Chair in Psychology reported to the Senate as follows:

> Private enquiries [since the interviews in that summer] have confirmed that there is not at present a field of candidates with qualifications suitable for appointment to a Chair of Psychology. The Committee understands, however, that in about two years' time candidates with suitable qualifications are more likely to be available.
>
> In view of this present dearth of candidates the Committee regrets that it does not expect to be able to make a nomination to the Chair for about two years.
>
> The Committee is of the opinion that a Department of Psychology should not be instituted in this University until it is possible to appoint a Professor of Psychology, and it therefore recommends that the question of the establishment of such a Department should be postponed for about two years.
>
> The Committee suggests, however, that the Faculty of Arts be asked to explore the possibility of providing in the meantime, within the Department of Philosophy, courses in Psychology sufficient to meet the needs of students in that Faculty.

It was probably expected that the two-year gap would be filled by additional experience on the part of individuals who had in recent years been diverted into military service, and who might apply for the Chair after that period. However, although the number of graduates with psychological training was increasing at this time, few had an academic career long enough to become a professor.

Following the committee's decision, a Lectureship in Psychology was authorised by the Faculty of Arts, to be held in the Department of Philosophy under the general supervision of the department's professor (B. M. Laing). Mr Adrian Gilbert was appointed in 1948. His contract was initially for two years only (because more substantial developments in psychology were anticipated; see above), but it was renewed and "established on a normal basis" by the Faculty in February 1950. It was at that point recommended that "if and when a Department of Psychology is set up, the Lectureship in Psychology be transferred to it". From October 1948 onwards it became possible to study psychology as one of three subjects for the General BA degree.

Adrian Gilbert had obtained a BSc from Birkbeck College, London, and had previously been employed as an investigator by the Industrial Health Research Board of the Medical Research Council. His approach to the subject was empirical rather than philosophical, and he had a particular interest in intelligence and ability testing. Publications included 'New-type examinations in technical education' (1951), and his research included studies of aspiration level in school-children.

These moves to strengthen psychology in the University of Sheffield after world war two were linked with more general plans for expansion. During 1943, a Development Committee had been set up to consider possible post-war initiatives. Attention was primarily directed at the need for additional buildings, to be constructed on sites to be acquired in the area. This task was given greater urgency by a request from the University Grants Committee in November of that year for estimates of post-war financial needs (Chapman, 1955). The university's Development Plan was submitted in April 1944.

It was proposed to double the pre-war student population (from about 750 to about 1,500 in ten years' time), through a general expansion of current departments[25]. However, one completely new provision was suggested, in the area described as 'social studies'. That was considered to include economics, statistics, psychology, social administration, social history and perhaps social biology[26].

Associated with the Development Plan, a separate School of Social Studies (not in any one faculty) was proposed, within which would be a new Department of Psychology. Extensive discussions took place about possible ways forward, which were complicated by the

---

[25] In fact, full-time student numbers increased from 767 in 1938-1939 to 918 (in 1945-1946), 1,374 (in 1946-1947), 1,704 (in 1947-1948), 1,910 (in 1948-1949) and 1,987 (in 1949-1950).

[26] A report to the Committee on Social Studies in January 1946 indicated that "the term 'social studies' is preferred to the term 'social science', since there is no such thing as one comprehensive social science, but only a gamut of very diverse forms of enquiry." In fact, the 1944 Development Plan had used the term 'science' rather than 'studies'.

failure to appoint a Professor of Psychology in 1948 (above)[27]. However, the School's first Director (Miss Ellinor I. Black, previously Senior Lecturer in Social Science in the University of Liverpool) took up her duties in January 1949, with the School's first set of (seven) students commencing in the following October[28]. Two qualifications in social work and social administration were offered: a post-graduate Diploma in Social Studies, and a Certificate in Social Studies for experienced social workers who had not previously obtained a degree[29]. The course content was similar in both cases, and both required training across two years.

The School of Social Studies initially conducted some work with the Lecturer in Psychology (Adrian Gilbert), for example jointly providing classes for engineering apprentices and Ministry of Labour staff attending the university for one day a week. Mr Gilbert also provided some psychology teaching to students working towards the Diploma or Certificate in Social Studies.

In 1946, the government's Report on Scientific Manpower declared that the output of qualified scientists should be doubled as quickly as possible, and universities were asked to reconsider their estimates of future numbers. Particularly great expansion was sought from smaller universities, including Sheffield. The University's projection of 1,500 students was increased to about 2,800 in ten years time, assuming that adequate funding would be received from the government and through a public appeal which was mounted at the time. Overall student numbers were thus to be increased almost fourfold from their pre-war level. The proposed new Psychology Department within a School of Social Studies fell within these general expansionary plans.

Although negotiations to acquire additional land had been underway since 1943, some owners in the neighbourhood were reluctant to sell, and an Act of Parliament was introduced and passed to permit compulsory purchase of some sites. This was the University of Sheffield (Lands) Act of 1948, and included 12 houses in Mushroom

---

[27] The person to be appointed to the new Chair in Psychology had been envisaged as the first Director of Social Studies. The failure to make such an appointment required a significant re-assessment.

[28] Ellinor Black died in January 1956. She was succeeded by Mr R. K. Kelsall, who had been Senior Officer in Charge of the Nuffield Research Unit at the London School of Economics since 1950.

[29] Degree courses were not provided in the School.

Lane and Western Bank. As will be described later, a Department of Psychology was subsequently housed on one of those sites.

2. DEVELOPMENTS IN THE 1950s: PSYCHOLOGY AND PHILOSOPHY

Psychology and the Department of Philosophy

Following the appointment of Adrian Gilbert as Lecturer in Psychology in 1948, teaching commenced through the Department of Philosophy. The university's Annual Report for 1948-1949 indicates that 13 students were registered for the first year of the Psychology General degree in the Philosophy Department, a figure that remained fairly constant over the next decade. General degree students took four subjects in their first ('Intermediate') year, and three subjects in later years.

David Cousin was appointed Professor of Philosophy in 1949, and contributed significantly to the early consolidation of psychology in Sheffield. For example, it was he who represented the discipline in meetings of the Faculty of Arts, where disagreements with classics, ancient history and language professors were not uncommon. Professor Cousin remained in post until 1969.

A second appointment in psychology was made in July 1955, when Geoffrey Pilkington took up the new position of Assistant Lecturer in Psychology. He had graduated in history in 1949 and in psychology in 1954, both those qualifications being awarded as external degrees from the University of London whilst he was a student at the then University College of Hull. After his second degree, he started a Research Fellowship at Bedford College, London, but that was cut short by his move to Sheffield in October 1955.

Adrian Gilbert died just before interviews for the second position took place. A replacement Lecturer in Psychology was quickly sought, and Dr T. P. H. (Peter) McKellar commenced work in November 1955[30]. His previous post had been as a Lecturer in Psychology at the University of Aberdeen. He was a graduate of the University of Otago, New Zealand, and had obtained a PhD from the University of London, with a thesis on human aggression. Among his publications was A Text-Book of Human Psychology (London: Cohen and West, 1952). Peter McKellar and Geoffrey Pilkington were together responsible for the progress of psychology in Sheffield up to the end of 1959. The

---

[30] Temporary assistance during this period was provided by David Crowther (Extramural Studies) and Reg Edwards (Education); also by J. R. Thompson, who, although retired from the Education Department, retained a part-time involvement.

former was promoted to Senior Lecturer in 1958, and the latter to Lecturer in 1958 and Senior Lecturer in 1967.

Linked to Peter McKellar's post was the appointment of a part-time secretary (Margaret Dobson) and a technician, who was shared equally with the Department of Education. Eric Eagle took up this post in 1956, contributing to the construction of experimental apparatus (primarily in wood and metal), developing photographic procedures for research and teaching, and attending to the rats held by both groups for research and teaching. The sub-section of the Philosophy Department[31] became known at this time as the Psychological Laboratory[32], acquired its own headed note-paper, and moved into its own premises (see below).

Animal studies were first carried out in the Psychological Laboratory by PhD student Roger Stretch, under Home Office approved supervision by Peter McKellar. Roger was a recent graduate from Nottingham University, whose project investigated operant conditioning and exploratory behaviour in rats; his doctorate was awarded in 1960. In addition to his activities as a research student, he was appointed a Part-time Teacher in Psychology in 1958.

Assistance was also provided by Charles Baker, who was appointed an Honorary Tutor in Industrial Psychology in 1956, becoming responsible for a new Behavioural Research Unit. He was initially employed with funds from the British Iron and Steel Research Association, and then from the Ministry of Defence through the Flying Personnel Research Committee. (More details are presented later in the chapter.) In addition to his research work, Charles taught occupational psychology as well as experimental design and statistics. He also organised part-time courses for local managers in industrial psychology, which were held in the laboratory. Charles moved to a Lectureship in Psychology in the University of Durham at the end of 1960. (Career details of staff are presented in Appendix 1.)

Contributions were also made by Pam Poppleton. She had gained a General BA degree in Economics, Philosophy and Spanish in 1942, and in 1957 returned to the university as a psychology student.

---

[31] The Philosophy Department (parent department to the psychologists) was itself very small, with only two full-time academic staff: Professor David Cousin and a single lecturer, Mr Wilfred Glasgow. Student numbers were also small, with only a single Honours graduate in 1956. Honours philosophy students were examined in General Psychology (two papers), as well as taking eight other papers.

[32] An entity with that name already existed within the Philosophy Department in the University of Hull, where Geoffrey Pilkington had studied psychology.

She was among the second set of psychology Honours graduates from the Philosophy Department (in 1959), having been exempted from one year of the course because of her previous qualification. She held a research assistantship between 1959 and 1960 (funded by the Ministry of Defence grant mentioned above), and also served as an Honorary Tutor in social psychology for that period.

Accommodation in the 1950s

Adrian Gilbert was based in a Victorian house in Leavygreave Road. That was shared with Accountancy, Law and Social Studies staff, and was later replaced by the current Hicks Building. Adrian had available one office and shared use of a small lecture room.

The university was extremely short of accommodation in that period, associated with a large increase in student numbers and a lack of funds for new building work. Temporary laboratory and office buildings were erected for some departments on the main university site in Western Bank, and others were adapted for new uses. However, the University of Sheffield (Lands) Act, passed by Parliament in 1948, permitted the purchase of more than 150 houses and other properties in the neighbourhood, and these had all been acquired by 1954. Among them were houses in the Mushroom Lane area, where the Department of Psychology and Institute of Work Psychology are sited today[33].

Two Victorian houses in Mushroom Lane (numbers 358 and 360, combined and interconnected) were occupied early by the Faculty of Medicine office. In 1947, the University's new Medical Centre (staffed by Dr P. W. W. Gifford and colleagues) was established, and this was also placed in that building. This joint occupation continued until 1955, when the Medical Faculty office took accommodation in Western Bank. The vacated space in 358-360 Mushroom Lane (on the ground floor) was made available for the new Psychological Laboratory[34].

The accommodation consisted of four offices for members of academic and research staff, a secretarial office, a larger room used for practical classes, and a small library which also served as a space for morning coffee and afternoon tea[35]. In the cellar was a room used for

---

[33]   Incidentally, the sports field behind these buildings was previously the New Dam (one of three), which was filled in just prior to the University's Golden Jubilee celebrations in 1955.

[34]   The Student Health Service (as the Medical Centre became called) remained in the building (on the first floor) until 1967, when it moved to Claremont Place.

[35]   The department's library contained books available for student borrowing, in addition to the more substantial collection held in the University Library.

lectures, one serving as a technician's workshop, and a photographic darkroom. Given that the numbers of students and staff were initially very small, the space provided in 358-360 Mushroom Lane was adequate at the time, although the lecture room in the cellar had white-washed stone walls, a very low ceiling and no windows.

Psychology Teaching in the 1950s

Teaching of psychology in Sheffield in the early 1950s was to three principal groups: students taking it as a first-year (Intermediate) subject; those studying in years two and three for a General BA Degree; and those working towards the Certificate or Diploma in Social Studies[36]. Both the Certificate and the Diploma (based within the School of Social Studies; see Chapter 1) involved two-year courses, the latter restricted to holders of university degrees. Psychology was only a small component of those courses, whose focus was on social work activities and professional issues, and the psychology staff's attention was mainly directed toward Intermediate and General degree students. All these were registered in the Arts Faculty, where the Department of Philosophy was located. In each year, there were about 12 Intermediate psychology students, about six taking a General or (later in the decade) Honours degree in years two and three, and about 15 Social Studies students[37].

Intermediate BA students had two hours of psychology lectures and three hours of practical work each week. Intermediate examinations were taken in May or June at the end of students' first year[38]. Psychology was only part of the first-year course, in that four different subjects had to be taken. Those were chosen from the following: Ancient History, Applied Mathematics, Architecture, Biblical History, Economics, English, French, Geography, German, Greek, Latin, Modern History, Music, Philosophy, Psychology, Pure Mathematics, and Spanish. At least one language other than English had to be studied, and either Latin or Greek was recommended in addition to English and other modern languages. University Calendars of the period describe the Intermediate psychology content as 'General and social psychology. The psychology of personality. Laboratory

---

[36] In addition, a small input was made to the teaching of medical students; see below.

[37] Most Social Studies students were registered for the Certificate, for example six in 1951 compared to only two Diploma students, and 15 of 16 students in 1956.

[38] Students failing an Intermediate exam were 'referred' and could take it again in September.

course'. Illustrative Intermediate exam papers (for 1954 and 1959) are presented in Appendixes 2A and 2B; students took two three-hour papers[39].

For the final two years of a General BA degree, two other subjects in addition to psychology were required. General degree students attended three hours each of lectures and of practical (laboratory) classes in psychology each week. The input was described in the university Calendar around 1950 as covering General Psychology and Social Psychology:

General Psychology: Introduction. Behaviour. Motivation of behaviour. The individual personality. Cognitive processes. Experimental psychology. Practical work.

Social Psychology: Introduction. Motivation of social behaviour. Psychological attitudes. Social induction of behaviour. Psychology of the group. Group mechanisms. The socialisation of the individual.

Appendixes 2C and 2D contain examples of final examination papers in psychology for the General BA degree in the 1950s; four papers were required.

The academic year was divided into three terms of ten weeks each, commencing around the beginning of October, January and April. All those weeks involved teaching in the first two terms, but classes ran for only about five weeks in the final term, with examinations occurring thereafter. There were thus usually 25 teaching weeks in an academic year.

The content of teaching in Adrian Gilbert's time is illustrated by the reading list presented in the Calendar of 1950-1951:

General Psychology

R. H. Thouless: General and Social Psychology. (University Tutorial Press).

R. S. Woodworth: Psychology: A Study of Mental Life. (Methuen).

R. S. Woodworth: Contemporary Schools of Psychology. (Methuen).

W. McDougall: Introduction to Social Psychology. (Methuen).

W. H. J. Sprott: General Psychology.

G. F. Stout: A Manual of Psychology. (University Tutorial Press).

J. C. Flugel: A Hundred Years of Psychology. (Duckworth).

G. W. Allport: Personality, a Psychological Interpretation. (New York, Henry Holt).

---

[39] The University's Intermediate examinations were renamed as 'First University Examinations' from the academic year 1965-1966.

Social Psychology
R. H. Thouless: <u>General and Social Psychology</u>. (University Tutorial Press).
W. McDougall: <u>Introduction to Social Psychology</u>. (Methuen).
W. McDougall: <u>The Group Mind</u>. (Methuen).
M. Ginsberg: <u>The Psychology of Society</u>. (Methuen).
M. Ginsberg: <u>Sociology</u>. (Home University Library).
K. Young: <u>Handbook of Social Psychology</u>. (Kegan Paul).
G. Murphy et al.: <u>Experimental Social Psychology</u>. (New York, Harper).
D. Katz and R. J. Schanck: <u>Social Psychology</u>. (Chapman and Hall).
J. Blackburn: <u>Psychology and the Social Pattern</u>. (Kegan Paul).

Many of those books had been published before the second world war. It is notable also that few laboratory-based texts were recommended at the time. However, both Intermediate and Final examinations in the early 1950s included practical tasks which required the application of statistics. Those examinations lasted three and six hours respectively; see Appendixes 2A and 2C.

An Honours degree in psychology was introduced from October 1955, despite strong objections from some members of the Arts Faculty Board[40]. The Head of the Philosophy Department (Professor David Cousin) faced opposition from representatives of the Departments of Greek, Latin, Ancient History and Spanish, whose conception of the Arts domain was very different from that proposed in the new course, with its strong empirical and laboratory emphasis[41].

General and Honours degree students attended together in the same classes, but coverage and final examinations for the latter were more substantial. From 1958 (the first year of Honours finals), there were nine (three-hour) papers in the Honours final examination, referred to as: General Psychology, Advanced Theory, Social Psychology, Genetic Psychology, History of Psychology, Physiological Psychology, Methodology, Personality and Psychopathology, and Applied Psychology. Examples of final Honours Psychology exams from the period (for the year 1959) are presented in Appendix 2E. In addition, Honours students had to submit a dissertation on a topic

---

[40] A joint Honours degree (Philosophy and Psychology) was also offered, but no students took this in the 1950s. See Chapter 4 for later developments.
[41] The study of rats and other animals in an Arts Faculty was considered particularly inappropriate by some members of the Board.

agreed with the department. This was carried out in the final year, and was supervised by a member of staff[42].

Emphasising the empirical nature of the discipline, Geoffrey Pilkington presented regular laboratory practical classes to first-year students. Peter McKellar was responsible for later practical work, mainly in the second year. Students were provided with background notes, references and guidelines, and wrote a report about each activity; this was marked and returned with written comments, although grades did not contribute to overall student assessment. Topics examined in practical classes included serial reproduction by a sequence of individuals, the measurement of the two-point tactual threshold, part- versus whole-learning, factors creating perceptual distortion, the measurement of galvanic skin responses, colour vision and other perceptual processes, personality assessment through inventories and projective tests, and the measurement of attitudes and values. Text-books included Experimental Psychology by R. S. Woodworth and H. Schlosberg, Handbook of Experimental Psychology edited by S. S. Stevens, and Social Psychology by D. Krech and R. S. Krutchfield.

Students were examined at the end of their second year, but performance at that time did not contribute to their degree classification. Subsequent to their final examinations at the end of year three, Honours students were required to attend for an individual oral (viva voce) examination, conducted by the External Examiner and (usually) all internal staff. In many cases, this was largely a formality (since a degree class had already been determined from exam performance), but for a minority of students the discussion affected a final grade. Individuals were informed that they might be placed in a higher classification as a result of an oral exam, but never in a lower one.

Teaching for psychology students was augmented by contributions from other departments. For example, Dr J. M. Thoday gave lectures in genetics[43], Miss (later Dr) Sheila Mitchell (School of Social Studies) taught statistics, Dr Peter Mann (Department of Sociology) added to social psychology teaching, and Mr Frank Girling (Department of Sociology) introduced some anthropological themes. Clinical psychology teaching was sometimes together with medical

---

[42] This framework of examinations continued until 1963. In that year, the dissertation came to count as two papers, and the number of exams was reduced to eight. See Chapter 4.

[43] Dr Thoday left the University in 1959, and became Professor of Genetics at Cambridge University.

students, through lectures and demonstrations by Professor E. Stengel (Department of Psychiatry). Other clinical psychological input was subsequently from Mr (later Dr) John Orme, who was appointed a Principal Psychologist in the Sheffield area of the National Health Service in 1958. Peter McKellar presented aspects of 'abnormal psychology', emphasising conceptual themes rather than clinical issues.

In the first three years of Honours psychology, six, ten and four students graduated (nine men and eleven women)[44]. Their degree classes were as follows:

	1958	1959	1960
Class 1	1	1	
Class 2, Division 1	4	3	
Class 2, Division 2		1	4
Class 3	1	5	

Psychological Research in the 1950s

Peter McKellar brought to Sheffield a concern for the detailed investigation of mental processes as well as behaviour. At a time when academic psychology involved almost exclusively the experimental investigation of behaviour, he focussed also on subjective experiences and motives in everyday settings, in part through a long-standing interest in Gestalt psychology and psychoanalytic theorising. He was strongly opposed to the philosophical behaviourism which at the time dominated American academic psychology.

His perspective was illustrated in his book Imagination and Thinking (London: Cohen and West, 1957; published in New York by Basic Books). This reviewed a broad range of psychological processes, both normal and abnormal, and described empirical surveys of types of experience as well as analyses of individual cases. Particular attention was paid to thoughts and experiences in psychoses, dreams and creative mental activity. For example, some studies examined hypnagogic imagery, vivid visual or other experiences of a quasi-hallucinatory kind experienced by some people when falling asleep. Others investigated synaesthesia, when a stimulus presented in one sense mode calls up vivid imagery of another sense; for example, an auditory stimulus may give rise to strong visual images.

In examining the similarities and differences between a wide range of subjective experiences, Peter McKellar included studies of drug-induced modifications. For example, he reported parallels

---

[44] Comparable numbers for the next decade are presented in Chapter 4.

between mescaline-induced and hypnagogic visions. He analysed the hallucinations occurring in 'model psychoses' brought about by chemical substances, and had a particular interest in the boundaries between normal and abnormal experiences. He also investigated the mental processes involved in time estimation, and chemical and other factors which might affect those. For example, oxygen deprivation studies were carried out in decompression chambers at the Royal Aircraft Establishment, Farnborough.

Peter had a strong interest in the strengths and weaknesses of different forms of psychological investigation. Geoffrey Pilkington shared this interest, and presented papers at this time on the nature of scientific method and explanation and the on characteristics of introspective reports. Papers with Wilfred Glasgow (Lecturer in the Philosophy Department) examined the concept of a soul, and with Peter McKellar reviewed aspects of inhibition in mental processes.

With funds initially from the British Iron and Steel Research Association (which was based in Sheffield), the Behavioural Research Unit was established in 1957 to investigate aspects of applied psychology. Within that unit, Charles Baker was particularly interested in human factors aspects of industrial safety and in psychological processes in technical change. For example, he carried out a survey of managers' attitudes towards human factors issues in the work-place. In 1958 and 1959, the unit was funded by the Ministry of Defence (through the Flying Personnel Research Committee) to investigate perceptual problems of map-reading through visual display screens, and Pam Poppleton undertook much of that work. In those pre-computer days, a simulated screen was created from wood and metal, on which lights could be illuminated at different positions by flicking switches at the rear.

PhD research in the 1950s was undertaken by John Tong, Kenneth Garwood, Roger Stretch and Ian Murphy. John Tong was employed as a psychologist at Rampton Hospital for mentally disturbed criminals. He examined relations between skin temperature and experiences of stress, and the patterns of recurrence of similar offences in criminal samples. He was supervised, successively, by Adrian Gilbert, Reg Edwards and Peter McKellar, and his PhD was awarded in 1959. Kenneth Garwood replaced John Tong at Rampton Hospital, and his PhD research (supervised by Peter McKellar) concerned personality, fear and anger among patient groups; his degree was awarded in 1961. Roger Stretch's project (also supervised by Peter McKellar) concerned curiosity and exploratory behaviour by rats; he was awarded a PhD in 1960. Ian Murphy had graduated in the 1958 Honours Psychology class, and (through a Medical Research Council studentship) investigated stress in aggressive offenders at Rampton Hospital (supervised by John Tong and Peter McKellar); his PhD was awarded in 1961.

Publications in the period included many talks given to local or national groups and (from the Behavioural Research Unit) reports to companies and associations. Some illustrative papers are:

Ardis, J. A. and McKellar, P. Hypnagogic imagery and mescaline. Journal of Mental Science, 1956, 102:426, 22-29.

Glasgow, W. D. and Pilkington, G. On the soul: A discussion. Mind, 1959, 68, 241-251.

McKellar, T. P. H. Scientific theory and psychosis: The model psychosis experiment and its significance. International Journal of Social Psychiatry, 1957, 3, 170-182.

Pilkington, G. W. Scientific method in psychology. British Journal of Statistical Psychology, 1958, 11, 129-132.

Simpson, L. and McKellar, P. Types of synaesthesia. Journal of Mental Science, 1955, 100:422, 141-147.

Psychology in Other Departments of the University

Although the primary 1950s development of psychology in the University of Sheffield took place within the Department of Philosophy, psychologists were also active elsewhere. Educational aspects of psychology continued to be explored, extramural teaching emphasised psychological issues, and medical education retained a small psychological component.

During the 1950s, psychological teaching in the Department of Education was carried out by Mr Reginald Edwards, who replaced E. J. G. Bradford on his retirement (see Chapter 1). Mr Edwards was appointed a Lecturer in Education in 1952, having previously been Educational Psychologist and Schools Organiser with the Rochdale Education Committee[45]. He had undertaken factor analytic studies of cognitive abilities, and retained an interest in methods of student and personnel selection. In recognition of his psychological background and teaching, his title became Lecturer in Education and Educational Psychology in 1956.

---

[45] Consistent with the limited availability of courses in the period, Reg Edwards had obtained an external BSc Honours Psychology degree from the University of London (in 1940) through a course of private study. He also received an MEd from Manchester University in 1950, while employed in Rochdale.

Psychology teaching in the education component of a BA or BSc General degree emphasised theories of learning and models of ability. Issues in genetics were covered, and there was a strong statistics component, taught by J. R. Thomson and later by Reg Edwards. Students attended three hours of lectures and up to six hours of practical classes each week. As was common at the time, practical work (supervised by Reg Edwards) sometimes involved maze-learning by rats or bar-pressing by pigeons, with a special focus on predictions from models by Tolman, Hull and Skinner. Practical classes also took place in local schools, for instance measuring children's body type, investigating their learning on standard tasks, or applying tests of intelligence and specific abilities. Students taking the Diploma in Education course[46] studied psychology as one of three areas (the others being the history and the philosophy of education).

In 1956, Eric Astington obtained what was probably the first Sheffield PhD with a psychological content. He was a school-teacher who had obtained an MEd degree from Manchester University in 1950. He carried out PhD research in addition to his principal job. Supervised in the Department of Education by E. J. G. Bradford and later by Reg Edwards, his thesis was entitled 'The influence of personality upon the academic achievement of grammar-school boys'.

In 1960, Reg Edwards moved from the Department of Education to a Chair in Education at McGill University, Canada. Pam Poppleton (see above) took over his role. As well as becoming a Lecturer in the Education Department, she was appointed an Honorary Tutor in Psychology at the beginning of 1961, and her links with the Psychology Department were strong for the next decade. Pam subsequently completed a PhD on the psychological correlates of adolescent change, became a Senior Lecturer in Education in 1970, and served as head of the Division of Education between 1982 and 1985, in which year she retired. However, she was active for many subsequent years in an honorary capacity in the division, for instance contributing to an international study of teachers' working lives.

Although the Department of Education provided courses for potential new teachers, those individuals already experienced in the job became the responsibility of a second part of the university -- the Institute of Education. That was founded in 1948, in response to a government request (arising from the McNair Report in 1944) that universities should be more involved in the training of teachers. It was

---

[46] The Diploma of Education was then a required qualification for would-be teachers.

operated jointly by the University of Sheffield and several local education authorities, with a headquarters in the university.

The Institute of Education did not provide instruction for undergraduates working towards a degree. It had two other functions: to supervise curricula and examinations for the Certificate of Education awarded to students in training colleges; and to provide for already-trained teachers classes towards the Advanced Certificate of Education. That was through a three-year part-time course offered to practising teachers in the area, which included psychology for all students in the first year and as an option in the second year. In the third year a dissertation was prepared, often supervised by Mr L. B. (Bunny) Birch, who was appointed a Lecturer in Educational Psychology in 1952. Mr Birch had trained as a psychologist at the University of Birmingham with Professor C. W. Valentine (see footnote 12), and came to Sheffield from an educational psychologist post at Burton on Trent. His contributions led to a strong psychological emphasis in the institute in this period.

Bunny Birch's publications focussed on the measurement of intellectual functioning, processes of learning, children with learning difficulties, and the application of experimental psychology to teacher training. He edited the British Journal of Educational Psychology between 1962 and 1967. In 1960, he was promoted to Senior Lecturer, and he moved to a Chair in Educational Psychology at McGill University, Canada in 1967. He was replaced by Dr Edith Richardson, previously a Principal Lecturer at Cartrefle College of Education, Wrexham, who held a degree in mathematics and a PhD in educational psychology. She retired in 1972.

Psychology was also taught from the Department of Extramural Studies in the 1950s, frequently to classes run by the Workers' Educational Association. Dr David Crowther contributed substantially to this work. Although primarily responsible for presenting classes on ethical and philosophical topics, he also gave courses on social relations, personality, leadership, child development, and other aspects of psychology[47]. Extramural psychological contributions came also from Reg Edwards (e.g., on child development, social psychology, statistics, personality and general psychology), from Adrian Gilbert (on experimental psychology), and from members of the new Psychological

---

[47] David Crowther died in post in 1963. He had been a Tutor (later renamed as Lecturer) in Extramural Studies since 1928, and contributed widely to discussions about psychological and philosophical issues across the University.

Laboratory: Peter McKellar on personality, social relationships and other topics, and Charles Baker on aspects of industrial psychology.

Psychological training for medical students at this time appeared in the curriculum both as 'normal psychology' and 'mental diseases'[48]. Teaching was at first principally through honorary contributions from local medical practitioners. For example, as summarised in Chapter 1, Dr J. Carson taught psychology up to 1957, and Dr F. J. S. Esher had broad interests in psychology as well as in psychiatry.

In 1955, the University appointed its first Professor of Psychiatry, Dr Erwin Stengel. With qualifications from Vienna, Edinburgh, Glasgow and London, his previous role had been as Reader in Psychiatry in the University of London. Psychological teaching to medical students was strengthened in 1956, when it became the responsibility of Peter McKellar. Associated with a gradual expansion of the Department of Psychiatry, a Lecturer in Clinical Psychology started work in 1959. This was Mr Peter Clarke, who was formerly an Honorary Lecturer in the Department of Medicine at the University of Birmingham. His responsibilities were primarily to medical students, but he also taught in the Psychology Department.

A New Department

As described in Chapter 1, the university had since 1946 wished to establish a separate Department of Psychology. However, few senior psychologists were available, and it had not proved possible in the 1940s to locate a suitable Head of Department.

Interest in the subject continued to grow during the 1950s, and informal enquiries were made about potential candidates. For example, in 1958 Oliver Zangwill, Professor of Experimental Psychology at the University of Cambridge, mentioned the possibility of a professorial position to Dr Harry Kay. A graduate of Cambridge University in 1948, Harry had obtained a PhD there in 1952 (thesis title: Experimental Studies of Adult Learning), and had been a Lecturer in Experimental Psychology at the University of Oxford since 1951.

In mid-1959, Harry Kay was invited to visit Sheffield to discuss plans for a new Chair. Also interviewed was Peter McKellar, Senior Lecturer in the Psychological Laboratory within the Philosophy Department. An offer was made to Harry Kay, who accepted on the basis that his request for an additional lecturer would be met. He took up his appointment on 1 January 1960, on which date a separate

---

[48]   This term was widely used in the Medical Faculty up to the mid-1950s, before being replaced by 'psychiatry'.

1950s Overview

Department of Psychology was created. Harry Kay became head of that department as well as Sheffield University's first Professor of Psychology.

3. 1960s OVERVIEW:
A SEPARATE PSYCHOLOGY DEPARTMENT

Members of the Teaching Staff

On the establishment of the Department of Psychology in January 1960, the teaching staff comprised Professor Harry Kay, Dr Peter McKellar (Senior Lecturer) and Mr Geoffrey Pilkington (Lecturer). An additional lectureship had been promised to the new department, and in the autumn of 1960 that position was filled by Dr Neville Moray, previously an Assistant Lecturer in Experimental Psychology in the University of Hull. Of those four members of the department, three were still in post at the end of the decade, Geoffrey and Neville having been promoted to Senior Lecturers in 1967 and 1966 respectively. Peter McKellar left in 1968, to become Professor of Psychology at the University of Otago, New Zealand.

Eight further appointments were made to the teaching staff during the 1960s, two of those being replacements, so that the Department comprised nine teaching staff in the 1969-1970 academic year. In addition, Dr Ray Kerry (a psychiatrist) and Dr John Orme (a clinical psychologist) were appointed as part-time Honorary Lecturers from 1966, and several graduate students provided assistance during the period with practical classes and other teaching activities. Part-time Honorary Lectureships were held by Dr John Annett (1961-1963), Mr Jack Clarkson (1962-1965) and Dr Peter Warr (1968 onwards). David Salter became a Temporary Lecturer in 1969 (up to 1971).

Peter Warr was appointed an Assistant Lecturer in Social Psychology in 1962, having previously worked as a researcher into learning and programmed instruction with John Annett and Max Sime (see Chapter 5). He became a Lecturer in 1964. Next to join the teaching staff (in 1965) was Kevin Connolly, becoming a Lecturer from a similar position in Birkbeck College, University of London. Kevin had previously been on the research staff of the department (1961-1962), working with Neville Moray.

Jack Clarkson was also appointed a Lecturer in 1965, with special responsibility for teaching and advising in statistics and research methods. Jack had previously carried out research in Oxford with John Annett and Harry Kay (see Chapter 5). In 1966, Adrian Simpson joined as an Assistant Lecturer, after two years PhD research into signal detection theory and attention at the University of Reading.

Two Assistant Lecturers were appointed in 1968. Christopher Spencer came from a Temporary Lectureship at the University of Reading, after completing a DPhil in social psychology at the University of Oxford, and John Frisby had almost completed his PhD studies of visual perception in the department. Those two replaced Peter McKellar and Peter Warr, who both left the teaching staff in that year. (Peter McKellar moved to Otago [see above], and Peter Warr became Assistant Director of the newly formed MRC Social and Applied Psychology in the department [see Chapter 5].) Chris and John became Lecturers in 1969. The final teaching appointment in the period was that of Dr John Davis, a clinical psychologist at Oxford College of Technology (now Oxford Brookes University); he became a Lecturer in 1969.

During this period British psychologists were much attracted to developments in USA, and it was considered desirable to visit North American centres. 'BTA' (for 'been to America') was occasionally jokingly applied as an informal qualification. Three members of the teaching staff spent sabbatical years in USA in this period. Peter McKellar was a Visiting Professor at the Highlands University of New Mexico in 1964-1965; Peter Warr was a Fulbright Scholar at Princeton University in 1966-1967; and Neville Moray was a Visiting Associate Professor at Massachusetts Institute of Technology in 1967-1968.

In overview, the department's teaching staff increased in the 1960s from four to nine, with additional assistance from one temporary lecturer and two honorary lecturers. In addition, the department came to employ a substantial number of research workers, almost all funded by grants from external bodies. Five people were in research posts in 1960 (John Annett, Charles Baker, Pam Poppleton, Max Sime and Peter Wright), and that number had increased to 17 by 1970. Student numbers also increased considerably, from four Honours graduates in 1960 to 39 in 1970, and from 3 to 15 PhD students (in all years of study). Those developments will be examined in the next two chapters, and brief biographies of staff and graduate students will be presented in Appendix 1.

The Departmental Strategy

The Department's strategy for teaching and research naturally evolved over time, and was not always explicitly formulated. However, Harry Kay frequently emphasised the interdependence of research and teaching, and he set out to create a department that excelled in both. He wrote in 1999 (personal communication):

> We took from the start that the best teachers at
> university level were the best researchers. Students
> should have contact with staff working on the frontiers.
> The aim was to give students something of what they
> might expect at the older universities. At the same time
> there should be throughout the department a buzz from
> other researchers absorbed in their work and eager to
> discuss it with all and sundry.

The main element of strategy was thus for research-led teaching
of a high quality. Associated with that, policies and expertise were
developed in the uncharted area of on-line computing. Computers at
the time were large and inflexible, working mainly off-line for
numerical computation or data-storage; none were used in Britain for
on-line psychological research. Sheffield was the first British
Psychology Department to install a computer for on-line
experimentation (an Elliott 903C, in November 1966; see Chapter 5).
A great deal of programming and interface construction was required
before this could be used interactively in experimental settings, and the
computer and its applications became central to the department's work.
Such a facility was unusual in the period, and the Sheffield Psychology
Department had a head-start on others in the country.

Much research (with or without the computer) had both a
practical and a theoretical focus. Harry Kay supported the position
taken by Frederic Bartlett (1886-1969), who had been Professor of
Experimental Psychology at Cambridge University between 1931 and
1953 and was an active Professor Emeritus until his death. Bartlett
believed that the most fruitful development of psychology depended on
its involvement in day-to-day issues, arguing that the greatest
theoretical advances were likely to come from researchers interested in
practical problems. He stressed that a theoretical perspective was
needed, but that this should derive from issues of practical importance
rather than from merely academic interest.

Harry Kay's position was spelled out in his Inaugural Lecture to
new colleagues in the University of Sheffield. Entitled 'The
Psychologist's Task', this was delivered in February 1960, very shortly
after his arrival, to a capacity audience curious to learn more about the
new department. The lecture ranged widely over links with philosophy,
psychiatry, zoology and statistics, citing examples of research into
animal (rat and monkey) behaviour, physiological psychology, skilled

human performance, and processes of learning. Those accounts were preceded by an introduction to Bartlett's work from the 1930s onward, which was identified as very different from traditional approaches.

> It was during and after the war that the Cambridge Psychological Laboratory under Bartlett turned to the study of skilled performances. A vast range of problems was tackled, including such studies as how fatigue influenced the piloting of aircraft, the effect of extreme hot and cold climates upon vigilance tasks such as radar watching, and the influence of age upon everyday skills. From the point of the research student, and I was one of them, this was a stimulating time, with the flow of ideas moving very fast. . . . . . . It was in this context that Bartlett imparted to his students the idea that not only could they contribute to the psychological demands of continuous technical change, but that in contributing they need not get lost in the ad hoc problem. Rather they could use such problems as stepping stones to theoretical questions. This is a live issue, but I have never seen the case so well presented as by Bartlett's laboratory. For these reasons I feel myself fortunate to be able to say with other British psychologists "I am a student of Bartlett". It is my hope that something of this spirit will persist in the teaching of the Sheffield department (Kay, 1960, p. 5)[49].

Of course, it would be wrong to suggest that all research staff and students continuously held before them this ideology, but, when generally characterising the department in comparison with others, this concern for both theory and practice undoubtedly marked out its special emphasis.

Another aspect of 1960s strategy concerned staff-student relations. Staff of the new department worked hard to sustain open and friendly communication with undergraduate and graduate students. In the earlier part of the decade, before more formal committee arrangements were considered desirable, informal relations were facilitated by small numbers and frequent contact.

---

[49] This research philosophy is also set out by Bartlett (1949) and Broadbent (1970).

The Departmental Climate

The notion of an organisation's climate, culture or atmosphere has received much research attention from occupational psychologists. Despite the presence of differences between individuals or groups within an organisation, a broadly shared overall climate can usually be discerned. That is most clear when comparing between different organisations, and there is no doubt that the 1960s Sheffield Psychology Department had a climate which was distinctive and valued by its members.

That climate changed somewhat in the course of the decade, associated with increasing size and formality and some shifts in student attitudes (see below). An overview is presented here, and more detailed accounts of teaching and research will be given in Chapters 4 and 5 respectively.

The atmosphere in the early years was strongly influenced by the young ages of the teaching staff; all were at first under 30 except Harry Kay and Peter McKellar. Associated with high levels of youthful enthusiasm, this brought a general willingness to work beyond formal obligations. For instance, students were occasionally accommodated by staff at home in times of crisis, and departmental meetings were regularly held in evenings at staff members' homes. The location of meetings rotated among the teaching staff, spouses prepared food, and discussion continued from 7.30 p.m. to 11 p.m. or midnight.

In the days of an all-male teaching staff, wives were much involved in social events and in entertaining student members of tutorial groups at home. For example, they often attended departmental parties (for both students and staff) subsequent to final examinations.

Some members of staff attended occasional sessions of the 'Oasis Dining Club'. Founded by Peter McKellar and Geoffrey Pilkington in the 1950s, this sought to locate and support satisfying restaurants in the locality. Geoffrey was himself Wine Secretary of Stephenson Hall of (Student) Residence, and his enthusiasm was transferred to many a wine-naïve new member of staff. Jack Clarkson later had access (as a member) to the Stephenson Hall wine cellar, and evening and week-end discussions sometimes took place in the Senior Common Room there. In addition, Neville Moray was Sub-Warden of Crewe Hall of Residence and Christopher Knapper was a Senior Tutor there, and Kevin Connolly was a Senior Tutor in Earnshaw Hall.

There was considerable social interaction in the department, and professional issues were reviewed informally as well as in scheduled meetings. Discussions over mid-morning coffee or afternoon tea were actively encouraged. Staff were expected to attend at those times, and students were welcomed, especially in earlier years. Coffee and tea were initially taken around the library's table, but, as the department expanded, more space for this purpose was required. A partition wall was then removed to open up together what had previously been an office and a corridor. The loss of needed office accommodation was considered to be outweighed by the benefit of more interaction space. In 1965, Peter Warr carried out a communication tracer study, to investigate the patterns of information flow in the department; the majority of material had passed through the coffee area.

Research seminars took place in the conventional manner. Each year those were co-ordinated by a graduate student, and were followed by discussions in a local pub and/or restaurant. In that period, cigarette and pipe smoking was common, and seminars or meetings involving certain members of staff (particularly Jack Clarkson and Peter McKellar) were renowned for their dense atmosphere.

It was customary in each year to organise a Finalists' Party, attended by staff, their wives and the graduating students. In the early years, this was held in Stephenson Hall of Residence, of which Geoffrey Pilkington was a member; venues in later years included the lecture room and other areas in the department. Christmas parties for staff and graduate students also took place in most years. Parties of both kinds included cabaret songs written by Jon Baggaley, Neville Moray and others, making gentle fun of people and events in the department. They were eagerly anticipated, as valued parts of the department's cycle of events. Several songs were captured on a 12-inch record, produced in 1970 by Jon Baggaley, of which 50 copies were sold to staff and students. Further details are provided in the Annex to this chapter.

Students' birthday parties were sometimes attended by staff. For example, in 1961 a 21st party for two third-year students was organised at Crewe Hall of Residence by Geoffrey Pilkington and Neville Moray. Wine was purchased for them, and calligraphed documents of celebration were prepared by the staff.

Cohesiveness was also encouraged through involvement, specially by graduate students, in what became the university's inter-departmental cricket competition. In addition, staff-student tennis matches were an important activity each summer, and meetings in pubs and elsewhere were common. The university's Psychology Society, run by students in the department, presented a thriving social programme, as well as arranging scientific discussions led by visiting speakers.

The situation for graduate students in the period is illustrated by these comments about the middle of the period covered here:

> My memories are extremely happy ones, and there is no doubt that the teaching, enthusiasm and sense of pioneering in the department were second to none. The whole building was buzzing with activity. Our social life was also very full, and included regular wine-tasting, boating on the dam behind the department, parties, evening classes with other students, and so on.

An undergraduate student in the department from the early sixties writes:

> There was a great deal of socialising that involved students and staff, and it was a wonderful environment to be an undergraduate. Even when the department got larger, this atmosphere persisted, although it was rather less intimate because of the growing numbers. I think the thing I most valued (though I articulated it fully only later) was being taken seriously by people who knew so much more than I.

A similar picture is painted by a graduate student from the middle of the decade:

> It was a great time to join the department, for it felt like a close-knit family. Life was centred around Eric Eagle's[50] tea-making ("you must let it mash") ritual, when all members of the department would meet twice daily. But, as we grew we fragmented. A faction would split off to attend to the needs of the new computer; more students needing more teaching left less time for departmental bonding.

---

[50] Eric was the technician initially shared with the Department of Education. He spent most of his time in the Psychology Department (with a workshop in the cellar), and in the mid-60s became a full-time member of that department.

Another graduate student reports that on arrival others emphasised that "this place really hums": "overall pervaded by a sense of purpose and getting somewhere, with numerous extra-curricular exchanges in corridors, homes, pubs and other places".

In respect of teaching and research, an optimistic outlook tended to view as readily achievable many goals that came to present obstacles in later years. For example, the department had no formal ethics committee in the 1960s. Studies of alcohol and risk-taking were undertaken without any outside review, and student members of practical classes examined cutaneous sensation by inserting needles into each others' skin or learned about the method of paired comparisons with different red wines as stimuli. Mild electric shocks were administered in a number of studies, and the facilities for animal care were somewhat below subsequent standards. External control increased gradually throughout the 1960s, and the earlier 'anything is possible' perspective became more cautious in later years.

Accommodation Developments

As described in Chapter 2, the Psychological Laboratory within the Department of Philosophy had since 1955 been housed on the ground floor of 358-360 Mushroom Lane, a Victorian building shared with the Student Health Service. The new Department of Psychology remained in that building, and additional space was provided during the 1960s.

From the outset, rooms were made available in part of the upper floors, to house the rat colony brought by Harry Kay from Oxford and to accommodate new research staff (see Chapter 5). In 1962, a temporary wooden building was constructed at the rear of the building, containing a single large teaching room. All lectures and seminars for second- and third-year students took place there[51]. A room on the ground floor of the main building continued to be used for practical classes for those students. The larger number of first-year students met in a lecture room in Western Bank and later in the Arts Tower (after its opening in 1965). Offices in 358-360 Mushroom Lane were available for single occupancy by teaching staff, but most research staff and graduate students shared rooms with others.

Minor modifications were made throughout the decade, including creation of the coffee lounge described above. One more substantial development was possible within the restrictions of space and finance.

---

[51] Before erection of this wooden building, lectures continued to be given in a windowless room in the cellar.

In 1965, a single-storey wooden block of ten offices was attached to the side of the building. This provided accommodation for teaching staff and research workers, and also (from 1966) housed the department's Elliott 903C computer (which is described in Chapter 5).

The inauguration of the Medical Research Council's Social and Applied Psychology Unit in 1968 (see Chapter 5) required still more accommodation, and two small portable buildings ('Portakabins') were installed (by crane) in the garden adjoining the main building in 1970[52]. Each of those provided space for four people.

In general, office accommodation for academic and support staff was adequate. Settings for experimental studies were more problematic, both in terms of their availability and their quality. Animal studies involved rats in the attic and chickens in the cellar. The 'rattic' was cramped (about three metres long) with a sloping roof, and its facilities were a long way from the research environment nowadays expected. The cellars used for research were small and dark, and a little frightening for those unfamiliar with them. One member of staff writes:

> I recall one day going down to the cellar to look for some more space to run experiments. We were working on imprinting, and wanted a quiet and secluded space to study chicks. We went into one of the cellars, which had not been used for a long time. The ceiling was low and infested with dirty cobwebs, but the most striking object was a giant bright orange fungus, about six feet long and four feet wide, which was taking over the cellar. I've never seen anything like it – it looked like something from an advanced science fiction film. Subsequently, we fought the thing to a standstill, and converted the cellar into a useful imprinting laboratory[53].

Research into behaviour genetics required space for fruit flies (drosophila melanogaster), and an area was partitioned off from office

---

[52] These are still there in 2001, although no longer used.

[53] The dark and dank attributes of the cellar area were exploited by Kevin Connolly and Peter Warr, who in 1965 launched a commercial venture ('Psalliota Systems') for growing mushrooms. Shares were sold to colleagues in the department, but the company's technical competence was lacking. Bankruptcy was not long delayed.

space to house those. Although that was satisfactory, the smell of peppermint (used in some studies to investigate selection for pro- or anti-peppermint preference) was not attractive.

Experiments with student participants were often carried out in individuals' offices. For instance, studies of verbal learning required the clearance of documents from desks, in order to present stimuli on cards to a learner sitting on the opposite side to the experimenter. However, in 1961 an experimental chamber (optimistically termed an 'anechoic room') was constructed in one of the cellars. That was a square area, with 'sound-proofing' provided by cardboard egg boxes attached to the inside of the plywood walls and ceiling. The modest success of this construction was impaired by the recurrent noise of footsteps along the main corridor overhead. (A specially thick carpet, bought later from research funds, proved helpful.) This 'sound-proof room' became more appropriately termed 'anechoic' in the 1970s, when a solid chamber with foam-rubber wedges was installed.

Some Societal Changes

The work of any one institution needs to be viewed in the context of wider developments. Three changes in Britain in the 1960s are particularly relevant to the Sheffield (and any) Psychology Department in that period: the Robbins Report on higher education (1963), the opening of departments in other universities, and (later in the decade) a broad-ranging challenge to existing values by younger members of society.

A concern for the role of higher education in Britain relative to other countries led the government in 1961 to establish a review committee, chaired by Lord Robbins. That committee reported in 1963, stating "unequivocally that – always provided that the training is suitable – there is a broad connection between the size of the stock of trained manpower in a community and its level of productivity per head" (Robbins, 1963, p. 73). A rapid and substantial expansion of university places was recommended, doubling the number of students in full-time higher education between 1959-1960 and 1969-1970, and increasing that number by more than three times in the 20 years to 1979-1980. This expansion was to include a 50% increase in graduate students, since the numbers receiving post-graduate education "are too small for the needs of the country and too small to represent a proper development of the intellectual powers of our young people" (p. 100). To cope with these increases, the Report asked for a substantial expansion of teaching staff, more than doubling their numbers between 1962-1963 and 1980-1981.

In addition to its concern for national productivity relative to that of other countries, the Robbins recommendations were driven by two 'demand' factors: a 'bulge' and a 'trend' (Layard, King and Moser, 1969). The 'bulge' resulted from an increased number of children born towards the end of and after the 1939-1945 world war, and the 'trend' was a continuing increase in the proportion of school-leavers obtaining good examination qualifications and likely to seek higher education.

The Robbins Report set out a detailed plan for expansion, including a five-year crash programme up to 1967-1968 to deal with the bulge. In practice, the increase in student numbers exceeded even the Report's recommendations, and changes in universities were both rapid and difficult. Not only were more students selected and taught, but increases in staff and resources had to be obtained and managed. The expansion of the Sheffield Psychology Department was part of that more general process.

Linked to the post-Robbins expansion, other universities opened new departments of psychology in this decade. That general development reflected a growing acceptance of the discipline both within universities and in society more widely. More and more positions in academic psychology and in applications of the subject (clinical, educational and occupational) were created. Universities found themselves in increasing competition for staff and students, and there emerged a greater tendency for individual departments to observe each others' performance and to learn from decisions taken elsewhere.

During the decade, new Departments of Psychology were established at the Wales University Colleges of Bangor (1963), Cardiff (1963) and Swansea (1964), the Universities of Birmingham (1965), Keele (1962), Leicester (1960), Newcastle (1966), Southampton (1964), Stirling (1967), Sussex (1965, in three separate schools), and at Goldsmiths College London (1967). In recent previous years, new departments had opened in the Universities of Bristol (1951, after an earlier closure), Durham (1950), Hull (1954), Leeds (1949), Liverpool (1947, after an earlier closure) and Nottingham (1959), and in Queens University of Belfast (1958)[54]. In many cases, some psychology

---

[54] Chapter 1 has referred to previously established departments in the Universities of Aberdeen, Bristol (to 1920), Cambridge, Edinburgh, Glasgow, Liverpool (to 1914), London (Bedford, Kings and University Colleges, and the Institute of Education), Manchester, Oxford, Reading and St Andrews.

teaching had previously been through a Department of Philosophy or of Education.

In parallel with this expansion of universities and of courses in psychology, the British Psychological Society increased its membership by two-thirds during the 1960s (3,051 members in 1960; 5,059 in 1970)[55]. This was the decade in which the discipline and the profession became established throughout the country.

A third development in the 1960s was of wider scope. In the second half of the decade (particularly from 1968 onwards) young people in many countries became involved in attempts, with similar general intentions and occasionally with violence, to change the values established in society (e.g., Blackstone, 1980; Rooke, 1971). A common theme was that contemporary power structures ought to be overturned. This was represented by issues and events of the following kind:

- strident assertions of radical philosophies that power should be allocated to lower-level members of any institution (employees in work organisations, students in schools and universities, and disadvantaged people in society generally).
- growing acceptance of left-wing political views associated with Marxism, Trotskyism or Maoism.
- demonstrations or riots to achieve more 'student power'[56]. An extreme view was that this involves "complete, democratic, control over courses, teaching methods and examinations, as well as the administration of institutions" (New Left Review, 1967, 44, p. 89). 'Civil disobedience' was justified because "students are an oppressed group, oppressed economically by the state and their parents, oppressed intellectually by the suffering weight of dead and conformist departments" (New Left Review, 1967, p. 5).
- student 'sit-ins' (forced occupation of university accommodation), and demands for open access to files about individuals' performance (sometimes leading to the opening of those files).
- forcible exclusion from university property of politicians and other speakers whose opinions were deemed to be inappropriate.
- an emphasis on individuals' right to self-determination, illustrated in universities by demands that students should control the curriculum and examination systems.

---

[55] There were more than 34,000 members in 2000.

[56] This term became popular by analogy to 'black power' in American civil rights demonstrations.

- a demand for self-government in student unions, in that their funds should be operated by members without influence from a parent university (e.g., in support of political activities).
- a desire for immediately 'relevant' education, rather than for more abstract or factual instruction.
- a wish to develop 'critical' studies in parallel with, or in opposition to, traditional approaches.
- a wish for more open and 'authentic' interpersonal relations, recognising and expressing feelings more freely.
- a growing availability and acceptance of drug-taking, linked to a general preference for immediate pleasurable experiences.
- the growth of a self-conscious 'youth culture', whose ideals were deemed by many to be more appropriate than traditional ones.
- the rise of 'student politics' as a major domain of activity within universities.
- sustained media attention to these events and themes, for instance, reporting and discussing demonstrations and riots from other countries (e.g., at the University of California at Berkeley or in the centre of Paris) as well as in the United Kingdom (e.g., at the London School of Economics).

These developments were associated with opposition to American involvement (from 1965) in the Vietnam War, objections to British rule in Rhodesia, and pressure for racial equality. A wide range of issues thus became the focus of protest within universities. "Vietnam, the Welsh language, squatters, Biafra, college bus services, Rhodesia, lodgings, Greece, refectory prices and Ireland have all made their contribution" (Rooke, 1971, p. 2)[57].

Student unrest occurred in Sheffield as elsewhere, and considerable time was spent in discussion, debate and disagreement, continuing into the 1970s. Some academics argued that the increasing problems arose from very rapid expansion following the 1963 Robbins Report (see above), especially in the social sciences. However, changes in the aspirations of young people and in wider societal attitudes occurred on an international scale and were subject to extensive media coverage and public discussion. Cultural change of that magnitude necessarily affected relationships within universities as well as elsewhere. Some consequences in the University of Sheffield will be considered in the next chapter.

---

[57] More general accounts (beyond the universities) have been provided by Fink, Gassert and Junker (1998), Gretton (1969) and Marwick (1998).

ANNEX TO CHAPTER 3

The audio recording of songs and sketches produced by Jon Baggaley in August 1970 contained "lyrics by Moray and Baggaley; improvised dialogue by Cook, Baggaley and Sewell; music occasionally original; pianist, Mr Edward Sweet".

It contained the following items: Down gay[58] friendly Mushroom Lane; Where do psychologists go when they die? The fastest reinforcement in the west; Experimentally speakin'; Wanted, a volunteer; Assessment calypso; Courtship songs of drosophila melanogaster; There's a little old department to the north of Western Bank; An artificial ear; Face to face; Alice's band (of secretaries); The HK song; Word of advice; Sweet and sour; A student is a student is a student.

For example, 'The fastest reinforcement in the west' was a 'country and western' account of B. F. Skinner's approach to behaviour and its modification, and 'The HK song' covered a range of habits and verbal expressions of Harry Kay.

---

[58] In 1970, 'gay' retained its traditional meaning as 'cheerful', with no allusion in the public mind to 'homosexual'.

4. TEACHING AND STAFF-STUDENT RELATIONS IN THE 1960s

Courses and Student Numbers

As described in Chapter 2, an Honours Bachelor of Arts degree in Psychology was first offered by Sheffield University in October 1955. In previous years, students reading Psychology within the Philosophy Department had all worked towards a General BA degree, taking final examinations in two other subjects in addition to Psychology. In all cases, they were required to sit an Intermediate Examination in four different subjects at the end of the first year, proceeding to later studies only if their initial performance was satisfactory.

As part of a common trend away from General degrees, Honours degrees in Psychology became the norm[59], so that the usual pattern of studies was of four subjects in the first (Intermediate) year and of Psychology alone in the next two years. (Dual-subject degrees will be described below.) From the 1965-1966 academic year, the Intermediate examination was renamed the First University examination, and the required number of subjects of study in year one was reduced from four to three.

After the creation of a new Faculty of Economic and Social Studies in 1959, some Honours Psychology students were registered through that faculty from October 1961 (rather than through Arts, as had been the case previously). Those students were required to study Economics as one of their first year subjects, and on graduation they were awarded a Bachelor of Arts in Economic Studies (BA Econ). After 1967, when the Faculty was renamed ('of Social Sciences'), its graduates obtained simply a Bachelor of Arts. In addition to registration through the Faculties of Arts or of Economic and Social Studies, some Psychology students were accepted through the Pure Science Faculty from October 1966, so that the department's first BSc graduates received their degrees in 1969.

As with most universities' departments of psychology, students' choice of faculty was determined primarily by their areas of specialism at school. For instance, pupils who had studied science subjects in their sixth form were able (from 1966, see above) to apply to the Faculty of

---

[59]   The Sheffield General degree was abolished in the mid-60s, when Combined Subject (dual or triple) degrees were introduced. The single-subject Honours degree remained the most popular.

Table 1. Overall numbers of students taking courses in Psychology: All undergraduate and graduate years together (from University <u>Annual Reports</u>, which contain this information only to 1966-1967).

Academic year	Arts Faculty	Pure Science Faculty	School of Social Studies*	Faculty of Economic and Social Studies*	Faculty of Medicine	Overall
1956-57	37		20			57
1957-58	42		27			69
1958-59	35		32		49	116
1959-60	41		26		50	117
1960-61	46		27		50	123
1961-62	50			35	62	147
1962-63	57			57	142	256
1963-64	64			71	160	295
1964-65	62			82	160	304
1965-66	66			112	159	337
1966-67	61	14		117	165	357

*The School of Social Studies became part of the new Faculty of Economic and Social Studies in October 1960. That was renamed the Faculty of Social Sciences in 1967.

Pure Science[60]. The required emphasis in the first university year also differed between the Faculty of Arts and the Faculty of Economic and Social Studies, with a focus on Economics and Sociology in the latter but not the former. The differential focus was made explicit in the University Ordinances about options available in choosing the three first-year subjects (four before 1965-66). Those options are illustrated in Annex A at the end of this chapter, for the academic year 1966-67. Despite that differential emphasis, students reading Psychology all followed the same syllabus irrespective of their faculty of registration.

Overall numbers of students taking any course in Psychology are summarised in Table 1. Those cover all years of study and include

---

[60] Before 1966, such students tended to apply through the Faculty of Economic and Social Studies.

post-graduate students. Contributions to the Certificate and Diploma in Social Studies continued only to 1961, when those courses were ended[61]. Teaching in the Faculty of Medicine was not substantial, being a single lecture each week to its second and third year students[62]. Apart from those in Social Studies and in Medicine, all undergraduate students taking Psychology were registered for Honours degrees.

Details of single Honours Psychology students and their degree classes are provided in Table 2 on the next page. Those figures concern single years of study (rather than all years together as in Table 1), and show an increase from six single-Honours graduates in 1958 to 29 in 1970. Comparable figures for 2000 are presented at the bottom of the table.

Overall, 40% of single Honours Psychology graduates obtained 'good' degree classifications (first-class or upper second) in the years between 1958 and 1970. In informal discussions in the period, the general expectation was that around 40% of Honours students deserved an upper second or first-class degree, and it is interesting that this was exactly the percentage awarded by the department. (Of course, a self-fulfilling prophecy may be operating here.) The pattern was probably very similar in other universities. However, the proportion of 'good degrees' has increased nationally in recent years, and Table 2 shows that for single Honours Psychology students it was 81% in Sheffield in 2000.

The table also indicates that in the earlier period the gender balance was approximately even (46% men and 54% women). In fact, the proportion of women was increasing throughout the years shown. By 2000, almost two thirds (63%) of single-Honours Psychology graduates were women. This trend has occurred throughout the country, with 75% of United Kingdom Psychology graduates in 1996 being women (Holdstock and Radford, 1998). There is evidence that the shift has been accompanied by a gradual change in the content of the subject to more 'feminine' concerns (Holdstock, 1998).

In addition to the single-subject Honours degree, dual-subject degrees were offered in the 1960s. From 1962, a dual degree with Philosophy was offered in both the Faculties of Arts and of Economic

---

[61]   The School of Social Studies became part of a new Department of Sociological Studies in 1960, with R. K. Kelsall as first professor.

[62]   Principal responsibility for teaching psychology to medical students passed to Peter Clarke, who was appointed Lecturer in Clinical Psychology in the Department of Psychiatry in 1959. He became a Senior Lecturer in 1970.

Table 2. Number of single-subject Honours Psychology students graduating in each year, with their degree classifications.

Year of graduation	First	Upper second	Lower second	Third	Total	Men	Women
1958	1	4		1	6	4	2
1959	1	3	1	5	10	4	6
1960			4		4	1	3
1961		2	3	3	8	6	2
1962		3	4	2	9	4	5
1963		4	2	1	7	4	3
1964		5	11	1	17	8	9
1965		7	6	1	14	7	7
1966		6	10	3	19	5	14
1967		14	11	3	28	15	13
1968	2	8	15		25	16	9
1969	1	8	19		28	9	19
1970	2	12	13	2	29	10	19
Total	7	76	99	22	204	93	111
Percentage	3%	37%	49%	11%	(100%)	46%	54%
2000 graduates							
Total	10	64	18		92	34	58
Percentage	11%	70%	19%		(100%)	37%	63%

and Social Studies. Students were required to have passed in both those subjects at the Intermediate level, and in subsequent years they studied only a portion of each single-subject syllabus.

For single-Honours Psychology students, the ten subjects of the final examination were from 1962-1963 as follows: Physiological Psychology, Comparative and Developmental Psychology, Experimental Psychology, Social Psychology, Personality and Abnormal Psychology, Design of Experiments and Statistical Methods, History and Theoretical Systems of Psychology, Essay, Dissertation on a subject selected by the candidate and approved by the Head of Department (counting as two papers). Finals papers for the years 1964 and 1969 are presented in Appendixes 3C and 3D.

Dual-subject students also reading Philosophy took five of those final psychology exams, in Experimental Psychology, Social Psychology, Personality and Abnormal Psychology, the Design of Experiments and Statistical Methods, and one of the following: History and Theoretical Systems of Psychology, a special subject chosen in consultation with the Heads of the Departments, or a Dissertation (counting as one paper)[63]. The five Philosophy exams for these Dual students were: Modern Philosophy 1 (Descartes to Hume), Modern Philosophy 2 (Kant), Logic and Metaphysics, Ethics, and one of the following: Greek Philosophy, Political Theory, a special subject chosen in consultation with the Heads of Department, or a Dissertation.

In 1964 a second dual-subject Honours degree was introduced, in conjunction with the Department of Sociological Studies. The Psychology content was the same as in dual studies with Philosophy (above), and the five Sociology final exams were in Sociological Theory, Methods of Sociology, Social Structure of Modern Britain, Comparative Social Structures, and Social Administration. The numbers of students and their degree outcomes are shown in Table 3 on the next page.

It can be seen that degree grades in conjunction with Philosophy were markedly poorer than with Sociology. That is probably due to the difficulty of combining the two approaches in undergraduate study, where somewhat different perspectives and criteria are applied in the two cases. Note that in these Dual degrees men were more likely to study Philosophy and women more likely to study Sociology.

Students entered the initial year of the course in one of two ways. First were those who had applied to the university explicitly in order to read Psychology, and would take the subject as one of the required four (reduced to three in 1965) in their first year, continuing with Psychology alone later. Those individuals had applied through the Universities' Central Council on Admissions (UCCA) to up to five different universities (and not all subsequently obtained the required grades in their Advanced Level school examinations), so that the probability of any one joining the department was low.

The second group of students taking Psychology in their first year had entered the university to read a subject other than Psychology, but were required to select additional courses for their Intermediate

---

[63] Towards the end of the decade, the options of a special subject or a dissertation were withdrawn for dual-Honours students, on the grounds that they required excessive time in a very crowded syllabus.

Table 3. Number of dual-subject Honours students graduating in each year, with their degree classifications (P with Philosophy; S with Sociology).

Year of degree	First	Upper second	Lower second	Third	Total	Men	Women
1965				1P	1P	1P	
1966							
1967	1S	1P, 1S			1P, 2S	1S	1P, 1S
1968	3S	15S	2P, 2S		2P, 20S	2P, 7S	13S
1969	3S	2P, 9S	1S		2P, 13S	2P, 2S	11S
1970		1P, 8S	1P		2P, 8S	1P, 1S	1P, 7S
Total	7S	4P, 33S	4P, 3S		8P, 43S	6P, 11S	2P, 32S
Percentage with:							
Philosophy		50	50		(100)	75	25
Sociology	16	77	7		(100)	26	74

Note: the Dual-subject degree with Philosophy was first offered in 1962, that with Sociology in 1964.

Examination[64] at the end of the year. Most of those studied the additional courses (e.g., Psychology) for one year only, but some switched into Honours Psychology at the end of that year. Decisions about these additional first-year courses were made during registration sessions at the beginning of the academic year, when new students met with staff to register in their primary department and to discuss with other departments whether they may join them for a single year. There was occasional rivalry between departments at registration, in competition to attract academically well-qualified students into their first-year course.

Advance offers about primary subjects were usually made to candidates on the basis of UCCA application forms alone, without any direct contact with an individual (but a few were interviewed; see Table 4). Those application forms (usually submitted in the autumn prior to an intended start-date) contained biographical and other information provided by an applicant, as well as evaluative comments by teachers. Of particular importance to university decision-makers

---

[64] Renamed as First University Examination in 1965-66.

Table 4. Numbers of students applying and registered in the Psychology Department in their first year (from a paper by Geoffrey Pilkington and Adrian Simpson, October 1970).

	1962	1963	1964	1965	1966	1967	1968	1969	1970
Number of applicants	85	93	126	267	425	587	766	601	657
Conditional offers	50	57	79	194	287	130	137	122	163
Unconditional offers	3	6	15	26	21	26	28	20	21
Applicants interviewed	15	14	23	20	3	3	1	5	5
Applicants registered	9	11	20	19	17	14	24	15	33
Total registered	51	54	73	98	92	80	68	60	80

was a head-teacher's prediction of an applicant's likely Advanced-level (A-level) examination grades. In most cases offers were 'conditional', accepting an applicant if he or she were to obtain certain A-level grades (B, C, C in the mid-60s), but for candidates deemed to be outstanding (or already having the necessary qualifications) an 'unconditional' offer might be made.

Prior to each academic year, the department was advised by faculties how many students could be admitted. Departmental staff responsible for admissions (in the period reviewed, Geoffrey Pilkington and (after 1966) Adrian Simpson), had to achieve that number on the basis of the UCCA applications and enquiries during registration sessions. The pattern of applications and outcomes up to the academic year 1970-1971 is shown in Table 4.

Teaching Content and Style: Undergraduate Students

In their first year, Psychology students attended two one-hour lectures and a three-hour practical class in each week (as well as studying two other subjects; see above). The lecture courses were for most of the decade entitled 'General and Experimental Psychology' and 'Personality and Social Psychology'. From 1968, they were identified as 'Experimental and Biological Foundations of Psychology' and 'Personality, Social and Developmental Psychology'.

Harry Kay was primarily responsible for the first set of lectures to 1960s first-year students. He provided a general introduction, to students most of whom would study Psychology for only a single year. A wide range of topics was covered, with the emphasis being on contributions from experimental psychology: perception, learning, remembering, and biological bases of behaviour. Students were also introduced to individual differences and the measurement of intelligence. Some lectures were given by Peter McKellar, Neville Moray and others

The first-year course in Personality, Social and Developmental Psychology was given mainly by Geoffrey Pilkington and Peter McKellar. Kevin Connolly and others provided input about developmental psychology topics. First-year practical classes were run by Geoffrey Pilkington, with assistance from graduate student 'demonstrators'. The classes covered experimental studies of perception, learning and memory, and projects about attitudes, abilities and other individual-difference variables.

Recommended textbooks for first-year students in the middle of the decade included the following. (Additional reading lists were provided for each course in the Honours years.)

Brett: History of Psychology
Hall and Lindzey: Theories of Personality
Hilgard and Marquis: Theories of Learning
Maccoby, Newcomb and Hartley: Readings in Social Psychology
Morgan: Physiological Psychology
Morgan and King: Introduction to Psychology
Rosenblith: Sensory Communication
Woodworth and Schlosberg: Experimental Psychology

First-year lectures took the conventional form, with audiences up to nearly 100 students (see Table 4). Some of those for Honours students (in their later two years) were more like seminar discussions, with smaller numbers (see Table 2) and greater interaction. (Degree of formality of course varied between lecturers and between sets of students.) Work in those years was oriented towards the final examinations, whose titles have been listed above, and examples of which are in Appendixes 3C and 3D.

There were naturally variations in teaching across the decade, linked to advances in the discipline, staff changes or periods of absence. Illustrations of lecture content for year-two and year-three students are as follows.

Physiological Psychology. This course was initially taught by Geoffrey Pilkington (as it had been in the 1950s), but responsibility passed to Neville Moray after his arrival in October 1960. Topics included the anatomy of the central nervous system, properties of nerve impulses, sensory systems (especially vision and hearing) and emotions. Reviews were provided of hormonal systems, electro-encephalography, sleep, and theories of cortical functioning.

Comparative and Developmental Psychology. Neville Moray discussed animal behaviours and physiological characteristics as a function of different levels of evolution. He covered ethological approaches to behaviour (e.g., in an examination of imprinting), different levels of nervous system and brain development, problem-solving and social behaviour in apes and other animals, and the comparative psychology of language. Kevin Connolly also lectured on this course from 1965, covering the genetics of behaviour, instinct and early experience, and issues of infancy, learning, memory, cognition and language.

Experimental Psychology. Harry Kay discussed research on skills, learning and remembering, examining processes of coding, input, storage and retrieval. Psychological studies of development and ageing were reviewed.

Social Psychology. Originally taught by Pam Poppleton (from 1960 in the Education Department; see Chapter 2), the focus was on the nature of attitudes and group processes. Peter Warr became responsible for the course in 1962, and he extended the content (in students' third year) to include social aspects of occupational psychology. Topics included sociometry, attitudes and behaviour, ethnocentrism, conformity, status, person perception, attitude change, leadership, theories of social comparison and cognitive dissonance, and explanations and research designs in social psychology. Third-year topics included the Hawthorne studies of interpersonal relations at work, payment schemes, restriction of output, participation in decision-making, supervisory behaviour, accidents, absenteeism, and informal interactions in organisations[65]. Don Rossi taught social psychology when Peter was absent in the 1966-1967 year, and Chris Spencer took over in 1968.

Personality and Abnormal Psychology. This area was primarily covered by Peter McKellar, who emphasised approaches by Spranger, Jung, Eysenck, Allport, Murray, etc., and deviations from normality as viewed primarily through psycho-analysis. The course also examined 'experimental psychopathology' induced through hallucinogenic drugs and environmental pressures. Clinical psychological input was

---

[65] Occupational Psychology was also taught in the Department of Extramural Studies by Sylvia Shimmin between 1963 and 1969. In the latter part of the decade, Sylvia also gave lectures in Social Psychology in the Department of Sociology. She later became Professor of Behaviour in Organisations at the University of Lancaster.

provided by attendance at classes for medical students given in the Medical School or at Middlewood Hospital by the Professor of Psychiatry, Erwin Stengel; these included the presentation of schizophrenic or other patients for general discussion. (Occasional visits were made to other local mental hospitals.) From 1966, honorary teaching assistance was given by Ray Kerry and John Orme (local National Health Service psychiatrist and clinical psychologist respectively). Peter Clarke, Lecturer in Clinical Psychology in the Department of Psychiatry from 1959, also contributed to teaching in the Psychology Department. Overall responsibility for the course passed to John Davis, on his appointment in 1969.

Design of Experiments and Statistical Methods. This was initially taught by Honorary Lecturers, Charles Baker in 1960 and then John Annett until 1963. Part of John's input was through a Skinner-style teaching programme (see Chapter 5). Jack Clarkson taught in an honorary capacity in 1963-1964, before becoming a Lecturer in 1964. Considerable emphasis was placed on non-parametric procedures, for situations in which the assumptions of normality underlying parametric analyses might not be met.

History and Theoretical Systems of Psychology. Initially taught by Geoffrey Pilkington, this course reviewed the origins of psychology in previous centuries, different schools in earlier years of the 20th century, psychoanalytic and other approaches, learning theories, and philosophical issues of mind and body. From 1966, Geoffrey presented to second-year students the 'History and Philosophy of Psychology', and Adrian Simpson covered in the third year 'Systems and Theories of Psychology'. The latter lectures described and evaluated work by Skinner, Hull, Tolman, Gestalt psychologists, Deutsch, information-processing approaches, and mathematical learning theory.

At different points during the decade, additional lectures were provided by staff of the university from other departments. For instance, Peter Mann gave lectures on aspects of Sociology and Frank Girling reviewed some elements of Anthropology.

Second- and third-year students also attended a three-hour practical class each week. Illustrative practical projects concerned experimental studies of sensation, remembering, psychophysical scaling, reaction times, and applications of information theory. For example, the Method of Paired Comparisons was taught by tasting six different types of chocolate (and once, disastrously, of red wine). Classes were taken mainly by Neville Moray and Harry Kay, with contributions also from Adrian Simpson, Kevin Connolly, John Elliott,

David Salter and others. Animal studies were included, for example of T-maze behaviour by rats, as was physiological work, such as dissection of sheep's brains collected by graduate students from a local abbatoir. Attitude measurement was covered by Geoffrey Pilkington, and aspects of conformity and leadership were examined by Peter Warr and Christopher Spencer.

With an increasing emphasis on empirical dissertation projects, practical classes in the spring term of the final year evolved into seminar discussions (rather than requiring additional empirical work). Topics were selected from options by groups of students, each of which made introductory presentations. Themes included psychological aspects of smoking, creativity and lateral thinking, linguistics, mass media, religious activity, and pollution.

In addition to lectures and practical classes, Honours students took part in fortnightly tutorial meetings with a member of staff or a graduate student. (There were up to 15 tutorials in an academic year[66].) Explicitly following the Oxbridge model, an essay had to be prepared in advance of each tutorial, and that formed the basis of discussion in the meeting. In most cases, essays were handed in before a tutorial and studied in advance by a tutor to identify topics for discussion. In students' third year, it became common to use tutorials for more general revision discussions, rather than restricting them to a single essay content.

Initially, tutorial groups comprised two students and a staff member, but, as the department became larger, a third student was included. Staff members met with the same students for an entire term, and thus had to lead discussions about a wide range of topics, not necessarily in their own areas of primary expertise. A more frequent change of tutor was introduced towards the end of the decade, after an initial term spent with a single staff member.

Third-year Honours students also carried out their own (usually empirical) dissertation project. Different dissertations ranged widely across areas, although the emphasis was on experimental or comparative subjects. Students chose their own topic, subject to departmental approval, and this aspect of the course was generally very popular[67]. All members of staff and a number of graduate students took on the role of supervisor.

---

[66] Dual-Honours students attended up to nine psychology tutorials in a year.

[67] Note that the dissertation provided the only opportunity for students to choose a particular area for study. All other parts of the course were standard requirements for everyone.

Departmental teaching, with its general emphasis on experimental psychology, was similar to that undertaken in most other departments in the country. Content and style were informally assessed by comparisons made by individuals serving as External Examiners for other universities. For example, Harry Kay examined undergraduates in nine other universities in the period of this book, and several members of staff also had experience as employees or examiners in other departments. The explicit intention was that the Sheffield Psychology Department's teaching was to be among the best.

Examinations

As was conventional at the time, almost all assessment of students was through three-hour examinations at the end of an academic year, with no prior indication of their content. Questions were usually variants of the 'describe and discuss' or 'compare and contrast' kind, in which candidates were asked to demonstrate both factual knowledge and competence in interpretation of the wording posed and issues explored in the literature. A general expectation was that a mere factual response deserved at best a lower second grade.

From 1963, eight papers were set as Final Examinations. Those were taken during two weeks in late May or early June, with one exam in each of several days. Seven exams covered the lecture areas described above, and in addition an Essay paper sought to assess students' broader understanding of the discipline and its applications. Requiring students to write more extensively than in other exams, a single essay was requested in a three-hour session, with topics chosen for their societal relevance as well as the scope they offered for logical arguments. As shown in Appendixes 3C and 3D (Paper VIII for the years 1964 and 1969), essay titles were single words or phrases. Example topics from other years include 'Stimulus', 'Mini-skirts', 'Novelty', 'Hypnosis' and 'Tobacco smoking'[68].

In addition to those eight three-hour examinations, students were also assessed through their dissertation project. Dissertations were given particular weight, counting (from 1963) as two examinations in the overall combination of marks. This double weight was unusual at the time.

'Sessional' examinations were taken at the end of the second year. Those were mainly to provide feedback to students (through discussion about their answers and the allocation of marks), and performance did not contribute to degree classification. Associated

---

[68] There were no practical examinations in psychology in this period.

with a growing interest in 'continuous assessment' (see below), second-year examinations became more important in the 1970s.

Students' degree classification in the 1960s was thus determined solely by Final Examination performance; each of eight papers contributed 10% to the overall mark and the dissertation project counted as 20%. This contrasts with the situation in 2000, when six modules were examined in each of two semesters in the second year (equivalent to 12 marks, each contributing 2.77%; 33% overall), and four modules were examined in each of two semesters in the third year (equivalent to eight marks, each contributing 5.55%; 44% overall). In addition, a third-year dissertation and extended essay contributed approximately 17% and 6% respectively.

Intermediate examinations (from 1965-1966 referred to as 'First University' exams) comprised two three-hour papers. Paper I covered issues in experimental, physiological and comparative psychology, and Paper II examined social and personality psychology and included a question requiring statistical computations[69]. Appendixes 3A and 3B contain the papers from 1964 and 1969.

Linked to a general increase in students' desire for change during the 1960s (see Chapter 3), many discussions were held from the middle of the decade onwards about possible amendments to the department's examination system. Any modifications would necessarily be slow, since they would have to be preceded by revisions to the university's Ordinances and Regulations. Such revisions required agreement at faculty and senate level, and reviews elsewhere in the university were proceeding at varying speeds and with differing degrees of enthusiasm.

Within the Psychology Department, informal discussions between individuals and groups were accompanied by debates in the department's Staff-Student Committee, which was established in 1967[70]. That committee was asked in 1968 to suggest how the current method of Psychology assessment might be changed. Recognising that opinions varied and that information was incomplete, the committee conducted a mail survey of final-year students' views. This was carried out after Final Examinations, but before the announcement of results.

---

[69] Students were required to obtain a pass mark on the statistics question, but that did not contribute to their overall classification.

[70] The department's Staff-Student Committee contained representatives from each group of students (including post-graduates) and two or three members of teaching staff. The Chairman was a staff member and the Secretary a student. The Committee met two or three times a term. It discussed practical concerns, such as library opening hours, coffee breaks, etc., and also served as a means for staff to explain current policies or proposals.

Thirty-five replies were received from single- and dual-Honours students.

Student opinion in many universities was moving away from unseen examinations toward 'continuous assessment' (a new phrase at the time), and this was reflected in responses to the survey. For example, 74% reported that they had not done themselves justice in Final Examinations, and 63% said they had experienced psychosomatic symptoms at the time (with 37% being prescribed sleeping tablets, tranquillisers or other medicines). Eighty per cent of respondents recommended in future some combination of examination methods, for example including assessment of practical class reports or essays written for tutorials.

Such a procedure was offered in the department as a voluntary option (thus requiring no formal changes at university level) from 1969-1970. In addition to the normal examination procedures, as described above, students were able to submit either four written pieces of work (tutorial essays or laboratory reports) or an extended essay on a topic chosen by themselves. The announcement of this change indicated that "the aim is to try and meet the legitimate point that students who think they have worked satisfactorily throughout the course may not do themselves justice in the final examination". This option was widely taken up, and was followed by a general move towards more continuous assessment[71] in the following decade. In the Psychology Department, this came (in the mid-70s) to include an 'extended essay' written in the course of a final year.

In accordance with nationwide procedures, external examiners served each year to monitor departmental standards. Those examiners commented on draft examination papers, and reviewed a proportion of the completed papers (all the papers in earlier years). They visited the department to discuss individual and overall results and to ensure comparability of standards between institutions. They met all final-year students individually, in what was known by staff as a 'friendly <u>viva</u>'; degree classification could not be reduced as a result of that meeting, and in practice it usually remained unchanged. As in the previous decade, individual students met with the external examiner and some internal examiners, to discuss their examination or dissertation content or topics of current interest. External examiners in the department up to the end of the 1960s are listed in Annex B at the end of this chapter

---

[71] 'Continuous' assessment was in practice 'course-work' assessment, being based on essays or project reports.

Graduate Students

Within the general strategy of a research-led department, graduate students (working towards a PhD) were an important group. Their research contributed to the overall body of knowledge, they assisted with undergraduate teaching, and they served as role models to students working toward their first degree.

A total of 36 graduate students worked in the department between 1960 and 1970. Most of those received funds through studentships (£450 p.a. in 1965) provided by the Department of Scientific and Industrial Research (DSIR), and the department's bids for two or three new studentships in each year were generally successful. Following the Science and Technology Act of 1965, DSIR was replaced by five research councils. Of those, the Medical Research Council, the Science Research Council, and the Social Science Research Council shared responsibility for psychological investigations, and all provided funds for PhD work in Sheffield.

In 1963, the Robbins Report (see Chapter 3) recommended an increase in graduate as well as undergraduate students (up by 50% by 1979-1980). That was justified by the need for more university teachers to cope with the general expansion and by the growing complexity of science, technology and social science. Changes in the nature of postgraduate education were also proposed:

> Postgraduate work . . . . . is frequently too narrowly conceived. . . . . There are general techniques and principles not covered by work for the first degree that need to be acquired even though they are not immediately useful for the particular subject of the thesis. . . . . We recommend that the kind of training by formal instruction and seminars provided by the best graduate schools of the United States should be provided for research students in this country. Except in rare cases, a research student should not be dependent for intellectual stimulus and training solely on a single supervisor (Robbins, 1963, p. 102).

Those themes were taken up by the Sheffield Department of Psychology, and a Graduate School was inaugurated in October 1965. This was a substantial innovation at the time, with no such schools in other psychology departments in the country. Clearly reflecting North American practice, it was advertised in the following terms:

> In psychology, as in so many of the biological sciences, there has been such a rapid increase in knowledge that that the undergraduate syllabus is already overburdened. Many subjects, in spite of their increasing contribution to research, can be taught only sketchily at the undergraduate level. As a result, the new graduate is often encouraged to specialise in a narrow field at a time when his[72] overall knowledge of the subject does not justify such an exclusive interest.

> The school will therefore have two complementary aims. It will give every encouragement to a graduate to carry out his own research, and it will provide him with the opportunity of becoming proficient in a number of subjects that are felt to be fundamental for academic and research psychologists of the future.

Seminars and practical classes took place during a student's first postgraduate year, and thesis research was later undertaken as usual. Particular emphasis was placed on computer programming and the use of computers, since "the increasing use of computers makes it necessary for future research workers in psychology to be familiar with programming techniques". Instruction in programming was organised by Thomas Green and Neville Moray, making it possible for students to use the department's Elliott 903C computer in their own research.

Other instruction in the Graduate School covered the design and construction of apparatus, including elementary electronics and circuit design (taught by Neville Moray and Max Sime, and later John Frisby), and statistics and experimental design (Jack Clarkson and later Adrian Simpson). Research findings and theories in psycholinguistics, information-processing, ergonomics, behaviour genetics, social psychology, imagery and creativity were presented by members of staff interested in each of those areas. Apart from computer programming guidance and practice, which extended across several months, other areas were covered in periods of approximately four weeks each.

The establishment of the Graduate School in 1965 led to a sharp increase in students working towards a PhD degree. The numbers of graduate students in the department (all years of study) were: 1960, 3;

---

[72] The use of 'he', 'him' or 'his', rather than 'he or she' etc. was customary in the 1960s.

1961, 2; 1962, 2; 1963, 3; 1964, 6; 1965, 11; 1966, 18; 1967, 24; 1968, 25; 1969, 22; 1970, 15.

The 1965 intake spent much of the first two weeks in group sessions intended to teach aspects of social interaction and interpersonal sensitivity in an 'experiential' manner. This 'T-group' (where 'T' stands for 'training') was based on procedures developed by Bion and colleagues at the Tavistock Institute, to make explicit processes of leadership and interdependence. Group members were asked to examine together their own feelings and activities in the 'here and now'. Initial sessions were marked by prolonged silence by the staff member (Peter Warr in this case), with a view to exposing for discussion issues of interpersonal dependence and authority.

The T-group had a strong impact, but not of the intended kind. One member recalled that sessions "were remarkable for their long silences, due to our reluctance to commit ourselves to anything definite. We all defensively clammed up, being almost total strangers to one another and feeling rather competitively sensitive". Another viewed the group as "a formative experience . . . . . which succeeded in provoking such antagonism that we instantly bonded into a cohesive group". It was replaced in subsequent years with group discussions that aimed to teach aspects of social psychology in a more conventional manner.

The more experienced members of the Graduate School contributed to the department's teaching by taking undergraduate tutorials and assisting with practical classes. In a few cases, they became responsible for lectures; for instance, Ian Horrell taught Physiological Psychology during Neville Moray's leave of absence (1967-1968), and Don Rossi taught Social Psychology during Peter Warr's absence (1966-1967).

Graduate students also undertook roles extending outside the department. For example, on the suggestion of Harry Kay, in 1967 they organised a national conference of psychology graduate students. This aimed to provide opportunities to meet fellow graduates, to discuss research projects, and to consider possible changes to post-graduate education. In addition, papers were presented by invited speakers Donald Broadbent and Norman Wetherick. Some 35 graduate students attended, in what was the first of an annual series of conferences now continuing for more than three decades.

The results of another graduate student activity were published by Smith, Ashton, Elliott, Freeland, Jones, McKinnon, Simpson and Strong (1969). Those individuals all entered the school in 1967, and together they surveyed sixth-formers' views about and attitudes to psychology. That topic was of special interest at the time, as the possibility of teaching psychology in schools (rather than only in universities) had recently been raised. Among the findings was an awareness by the school pupils studied that psychology was both a science and an arts discipline.

The Graduate School in Psychology was very successful, both in its intended purposes and in presenting an image of the department as a national leader in psychological research and education. In 1969, slight changes were introduced, recognising that the students most valued instruction in techniques with general application rather than the presentation of specific findings or theories. From 1970, three compulsory courses were offered: computing (on- and off-line), statistics and experimental design, and equipment and materials. In addition, students were required to attend specialist courses outside their own area, selected in consultation with their supervisor.

Relations between Staff and Students

Commencing around the middle of the 1960s, many students in British universities became concerned for greater influence, freedom and self-expression. Linked to the broader social trends outlined at the end of Chapter 3, relations between staff and students became generally less positive.

Harry Kay was involved in these developments within the university as a whole, being (from 1963 to 1966) Chairman of a newly-formed Academic Development Committee[73] and (from 1967) a Pro-Vice-Chancellor. He was thus in a position both to bring to the Psychology Department new ideas emerging elsewhere in the university and also to advocate those procedures and values considered appropriate by his departmental colleagues.

The University of Sheffield spent a considerable time (for instance, in Senate or the Faculty Boards) in discussions about possible changes in decision-making to allow greater student participation. Those were influenced by a general national concern, and by widespread publicity given to student demonstrations against perceived maltreatment. The protest movement was linked to objections to US policy in the Vietnam War, and a concern to 'make love not war' through for instance what was characterised as 'flower power'. (See the final section of Chapter 3.) A specific legal change arose from the Latey Committee Report of 1967, that the age of majority (for example,

---

[73] There were nine committee members (all members of Senate) and the Vice-Chancellor.

in parliamentary elections) should be reduced from 21 to 18. That meant that universities became absolved from their duty to care for students in loco parentis, and the report was regarded as a national acceptance of the need to offer increased responsibility to young people.

Discussions took place between the Committee of Vice-Chancellors and Principals and the National Union of Students, leading to a Joint Statement in October 1968, recommending for universities as a whole greater student participation in decision-making. It was advocated that this should be substantial in matters of student welfare, and also cover (but with final authority held by staff) issues of curriculum, examinations and general educational principles.

In Sheffield, a special 'informal' meeting of Senate in September 1968 reviewed the local situation and considered possible ways forward. Students were by then equally represented on the university's Staff-Student Committee, and that arrangement was considered to be effective. Across the university as a whole, some 17 committees or sub-committees had a number of students as members. It was agreed in subsequent meetings of Senate that some student involvement in the working of Senate would be appropriate, at first through 'observers' (with the right to speak but not vote) but from 1972-73 as full members (also of the University Council). However, a procedure for 'reserved areas' of discussion was introduced, whereby student members could be excluded on the decision of the Chairman at the time. A general movement occurred in the university towards greater student involvement, for example through the establishment of staff-student committees in every department[74].

A minority of students favoured 'direct action' to achieve change. For example, a small number interrupted a talk by the Vice-Chancellor in late 1967, demanding a discussion on topics of their choosing. (Their demand was placed before the full audience, receiving only a minority of votes.) On another occasion, the Vice-Chancellor responded to a plan for students to forcibly occupy administrative offices and examine personal files by proposing a university-wide vote on the issue; overall not many students were in favour. In November 1968, the Students' Union forbade its Conservative Association to invite the politician Enoch Powell to address it (on the grounds that his safety could not be guaranteed). There was thus a widespread testing of

---

[74] As in organisations in general, this emphasis on participation by individuals low in the hierarchy presented problems for others in the middle of that hierarchy. Thus junior academic and other staff sometimes felt excluded by the changes introduced.

the limits of authority, with some students working to reduce the discretionary power held by other individuals or groups.

Relationships in the Psychology Department did not become as strained as in some other parts of the university. In the early part of the decade, informal contact was encouraged by the small numbers of students, and their frequent meetings with staff at coffee or tea breaks, in practical classes and tutorials, and in sporting and social events. Increasing numbers of students, and the general changes in outlook, led to establishment in the department of a Staff-Student Committee in 1967 (see above).

Methods to assess student performance were of considerable concern to this committee, as they were more generally, and different possible changes were reviewed. At the time, degree classifications were determined entirely by performance in 'unseen' examinations taken at the end of students' third year. Some student members of the Staff-Student Committee argued for the replacement of these final examination papers by self-assessment by students. It was proposed that only in cases where that self-assessment differed from a classification by staff would a student need to sit examinations. This proposal raised the general issue of how staff might appraise student performance prior to final exams within the current procedures. Furthermore, changes of this kind would require approval by Senate, and implementation could not be for three further years (being in place at the outset of a student's course). The proposals were not pursued, but the discussions were important in opening up consideration of alternative assessment methods.

Also of concern at the time was the accessibility of student records. These contained information about a student's initial application to the university, examination results in each year, and other information about performance provided by tutors and others. Although some students proposed that these documents should be publicly available, that was resisted by staff. The latter argued that material in the records had to be confidential in order to preserve its value; 'open' records would be likely to contain only partial information, since staff would not wish some material to be subject to public discussion. In addition, many students did not want their own records to be available to others. In some universities students used force to obtain access to records, but no such attempts were made in the Department of Psychology. More generally, no physical attacks on staff or disruption of teaching occurred.

Towards the end of the decade, some Psychology students sought to determine the content of their courses, but this desire was usually not of long duration. For example, some members of the Experimental Psychology class asked to select the topics for consideration; the request was accepted, and issues such as witchcraft and transcendentalism were placed on the agenda. However, after only a few weeks the majority sought a return to a conventional syllabus.

Many students were enthusiastic about currently-popular ideas of 'humanistic' psychology, arguing that experimental or physiological approaches downgraded the person. The relative appropriateness of a 'scientific' perspective on people (viewed by some as cold, artificial and demeaning, and by others as the basis for improving health and welfare) or a 'humanistic' approach (seen by some as authentic and validating, and by others as warm, cuddly and ineffective) was much discussed.

As elsewhere, students differed in their wish for change. In the university as a whole, a very small number viewed violent action as an appropriate means toward their ends, but the large majority aspired in a peaceful manner to have a greater voice in matters of concern to them[75]. Within the Psychology Department, almost all students were opposed to violence, and discussions were maintained through the Staff-Student Committee. Considerable time was spent in formal and informal staff meetings to discuss student attitudes and concerns. Relationships in the department remained polite and often friendly. Staff believed that students taking a dual degree with Sociology were more likely to propose radical changes than were single-subject Psychology students, perhaps because of different self-selection into the two courses. A very small number of graduate students appeared motivated by political interests, and sought to influence radically the department's structure and procedures. However, their impact was limited and brief.

ANNEX A TO CHAPTER 4

Requirements for the First University Examination[76] in 1966-1967
Students were required to study three subjects in their first year, depending on their faculty of registration. For those in the Psychology

---

[75]   A much publicised student riot in Paris in 1968 led to increased pressure for violent activity in some quarters.
[76]   Referred to as the Honours Qualifying Examination in the Faculty of Pure Science.

Department, two other subjects were thus required, drawn from the following lists.

Faculty of Arts

Ancient History, Applied Mathematics, Architecture, Biblical History and Literature, Economics, Economic History, English, French, Geography, German, Greek, Latin, Modern English History, Modern European History, Music, Italian, Philosophy, Political Theory and Institutions, Prehistory and Archaeology, Psychology, Pure Mathematics, Russian, Spanish.

Faculty of Pure Science

Biochemistry, Biology, Chemistry, Geography, Geology, Mathematics, Physics, Psychology, Statistics.

Faculty of Economic and Social Studies

Two from List A and one from List B below:

List A

Accountancy and Financial Administration, Economic History, Economics, Geography, Political Theory and Institutions, Psychology, Sociology.

List B

Accountancy and Financial Administration, Economic History, Economics, English, French, Genetics, Geography, Geology, German, Modern English History, Modern European History, Italian, Law, Political Theory and Institutions, Philosophy, Physiology, Psychology, Pure Mathematics, Sociology, Spanish, Statistics.

("A candidate who does not offer Statistics as one of his [sic] three subjects must in addition pursue an introductory course in the Elements of Statistical Method.")

ANNEX B TO CHAPTER 4

External Examiners in the Sheffield Psychology Department to 1971

1952-1954: Alec Rodger, Reader in Psychology, Birkbeck College, University of London.

1955-1957: John Cohen, Professor of Psychology, University of Manchester.

1958-1960: Rex Knight, Professor of Psychology, University of Aberdeen.

1961-1962: Jacek Szafran, Lecturer in Psychology, University of Exeter.

1963-1965:   Alan Watson, Lecturer in Experimental Psychology, University of Cambridge.

1966-1968: Brian Foss, Professor of Educational Psychology, Institute of Education, University of London.

1969-1971: Ian Hunter, Professor of Psychology, University of Keele.

5. PRINCIPAL RESEARCH THEMES IN THE 1960s

Research excellence was a central objective in the new department's strategy. Throughout the 1960s, substantial research grants were obtained from government and other sources and an active post-graduate research culture was created. Aspects of the department's studies are summarised here, under the broad category labels applied at the time. The principal focus is on research funded by grants awarded to members of the teaching staff, rather than the work of individual students.

In the first half of the decade, most statistical analyses of research data were carried out on mechanical calculating machines, cranking a lever on the right-hand side and obtaining printed calculations on a paper tape. A few analyses employed the university's LEO mainframe computer[77] (with long paper tapes or punched cards), but by the end of the decade the department's own smaller computer was available for statistical as well as experimental work.

Experimental Psychology

Staff and graduate students working in this area in the 1960s included John Annett, Jon Baggaley, John Bradshaw, Jack Clarkson, Ian Davies, Bob Dudley, Mike Fitter, John Frisby, Thomas Green, Godfrey Harrison, Ian Horrell, Michael Howe, Ann Jordan, Harry Kay, David Marks, Neville Moray, Rex Newsome, David Salter, Max Sime, Adrian Simpson, Richard Strong, Geoffrey Underwood, Peter Warr and Ed Whelan[78].

The term 'experimental' was used in the 1960s much as 'cognitive' is used at present, with a focus on laboratory investigations of perception, learning and memory. Departmental projects of that kind are illustrated here[79].

---

[77] 'LEO' was an abbreviation of 'Lyons Electronic Office'. The British catering company J. Lyons created the world's first business computer in 1950, and subsequently marketed this through its subsidiary Leo Computing.

[78] Further information about individual members of the department is provided in Appendix 1. Research topics examined by graduate students are indicated there.

[79] Note that some investigations presented in later sections might also be considered as instances of 'experimental' psychology.

Neville Moray examined aspects of selective auditory attention, in part through shadowing experiments and (later in the decade) two-channel attention psychophysics. The aim was to specify more closely the processes of selective attention: what factors influence how people can attend to one stimulus rather than another, and in what circumstances does attention break down? For example, in some studies listeners were presented with different word sequences simultaneously to both ears, and asked to report what they had heard. It was found that, with very short gaps between consecutive items (but not with longer gaps), words from one ear were likely to be reported before those from the other. These projects were funded by grants from the Ministry of Defence (1962-1965) and the Science Research Council (1968-1971).

With funds from the US Navy (1962-1963), John Annett and Jack Clarkson examined the role of feedback in a range of auditory discrimination tasks. In addition to its scientific interest, this work had practical implications for sonar operators seeking to distinguish between stimuli from submarines and underwater creatures. The themes were later extended by other staff into studies of feedback in learning and information-processing of several kinds. For instance, one study examined the content and process of emitted speech as a function of feedback quality.

Other experimental studies were by Peter Warr, examining the effect of repetition of material on its learning and retention. A topical issue at the time was the possibility of 'all-or-none' learning of verbal associations, such that presentation of material led to the formation of either a strong association or no association at all. By replacing learned paired associate items on a given trial with completely new items on the next trial, it was possible to examine the covariation between number of presentations and the probability of a correct response[80]. Additional studies explored the possibility that paired associate learning occurred in two phases, observing that all-or-none learning was particularly likely in one of those phases (the acquisition of responses rather than of associations). The effect of varying amount of repetition was also investigated as a function of task difficulty. These studies were funded by the Department of Scientific and Industrial Research (1961-1963).

---

[80] Before the availability of on-line computers, performance-dependent presentation of material to be learned (stencilled on cards) had to be achieved by rapid decision-making about the correctness of a response and some dexterity in uncovering a new stimulus card when appropriate.

Research by Thomas Green (in an IBM Fellowship between 1965 and 1968) examined the role of syntactic knowledge in sentence perception. Using simulated grammars, he carried out experiments to investigate how semantic-free learning was affected by distortions in grammar and how knowledge of grammar assisted in the perception and learning of new material. Thomas subsequently worked with Max Sime on SSRC-funded studies of time and errors in choice-reaction tasks, using the department's computer system acquired in 1966 (see below). For example, reactions to presented stimuli were timed, and subsequent presentations were based upon the speed of earlier ones: stimuli with longer reaction times were more frequently repeated, thus enhancing learning. This on-line adaptability was a novel procedure at the time, not possible with traditional apparatus.

Other investigations under the 'experimental' heading were linked to research grants described later in the chapter. For example, within an SSRC grant to Neville Moray and Harry Kay (Auto-Instructional Methods in Industrial Training, 1963-1967), research investigated practice effects in the storage of multi-dimensional stimuli and the effects of cueing on the acquisition of serial lists. As part of this work, Godfrey Harrison and Max Sime varied presentation content as a function of previous performance (e.g., in learning piano chords or serial lists), to explore the impact of different forms of feedback.

John Frisby's PhD studies investigated whether the then recently published findings of Hubel and Wiesel, on orientationally tuned cells in the visual cortex, could be related to mechanisms supporting human motion perception. Assisted by Rex Newsome, he constructed a three-field tachistoscope and examined orientational tuning of the phi-phenomenon, with positive results. He later pursued a similar line of enquiry for stereoscopic vision.

Some publications during the decade were:

Clarkson, J. K. Proactive inhibition as an artefact of the method of paced anticipation. Quarterly Journal of Experimental Psychology, 1967, 19, 49-53.

Harrison, G. J. Some additive results in short-term memory. Acta Psychologica, 1967, 27, 306-315.

Howe, M. J. Intra-list differences in short-term memory. Quarterly Journal of Experimental Psychology, 1965, 17, 338-342.

Kay, H. Theories of aging and learning. In J. E. Birren (ed.), Handbook of Aging and the Individual. Chicago: University of Chicago Press.

Kay, H. and Weiss, A. D. Relationship between simple and serial reaction times. Nature, 1961, 191, 790-791.

Moray, N. Broadbent's filter theory: Postulate H and the problem of shifting time. Quarterly Journal of Experimental Psychology, 1960, 12, 214-221.

Moray, N. Perceptual defence and filter theory. Nature, 1961, 191, 940.

Moray, N. Where is capacity limited? A survey and a model. Acta Psychologica, 1967, 27, 84-93.

Moray, N. Time sharing in auditory perception: Effect of stimulus duration. Journal of the Acoustical Society of America, 1970, 47, 660-661.

Moray, N., Barnett, T and Bates, A. Experiments on the four-eared man. Journal of the Acoustical Society of America, 1965, 38, 196-201.

Moray, N. and Jordan, A. Practice and compatibility in two-channel short-term memory. Psychonomic Science, 1966, 4, 427-428.

Simpson, A. J. Some studies of signal detection in vigilance. Bulletin of the British Psychological Society, 1967, 20, 10.

Warr, P. B. The effect of repeated presentation of items on paired associate learning. Quarterly Journal of Experimental Psychology, 1963, 15, 262-272.

Warr, P. B. The relative importance of proactive inhibition and degree of learning in retention of paired associate items. British Journal of Psychology, 1964, 55, 19-30.

Comparative[81] and Physiological Psychology

Staff and graduate students working in this area in the 1960s included Paul Arnold, Kevin Connolly, Robert Cook, John Elliott, Harry Kay, Neville Moray, Hilary Oldfield-Box, David Sewell and Peter Wright.

Several issues in this broad area were examined in the department's first decade. For instance, Harry Kay extended his interest in age and learning through studies of reversal learning in rats,

---

[81] Relatively little work on 'comparative' psychology has entailed comparisons between species. More commonly, animals have been used for practical reasons, but with an implicit assumption that studies might provide a model for other species, especially humans. The term 'comparative psychology' has now been largely replaced by 'animal behaviour', 'behavioural ethology' or 'ethology'. (I am grateful to Kevin Connolly for material in this section.)

in collaboration with Hilary Oldfield-Box, Max Sime and Peter Wright. This research arose partly from previous studies of human learning, which had pointed to older people's difficulty in correcting mistakes made earlier. The experiments with rats manipulated the content of problems, so that previous learning became inappropriate and was likely to generate interference. Comparisons were made between the ability of older and younger rats to solve an initial discrimination problem, to learn to reverse the responses that had been established, and to improve performance in subsequent reversals. Significant variations were found between specific experimental conditions, but few differences occurred between the performance of older and younger animals.

Other studies with the department's rat colony were designed to examine the social division of labour, distinguishing between 'workers' and 'parasites'. Hilary Oldfield-Box used operant learning techniques to investigate the acquisition of food attainment by rats as a group, tracing across time the creation and stabilisation of social structures.

In 1960, a new sub-discipline of 'behaviour genetics' was beginning to emerge in behavioural biology. The 'nature-nurture' controversy was of great interest, and biologists tended to emphasise the contribution that behaviour played in evolution. With a grant from the Medical Research Council (1961-1963), Neville Moray and Kevin Connolly (and subsequently Paul Arnold) carried out a series of experiments with fruit flies (drosophila melanogaster). The initial study sought to manipulate an aversive response (to the odour of peppermint) by genetic selection for and against the avoiding response. It was found possible to change some behavioural characteristics permanently, so that, even when selection pressure was removed, flies retained the changed characteristics.

Grants to Kevin from the Kittay Foundation of New York and the Medical Research Council permitted the extension of this work. In one experiment, flies were selected across generations for increased or decreased activity, yielding two lines that differed markedly for this behavioural characteristic. The two activity lines were found subsequently to show differences in their mating preference. The active females, when offered a choice of active or inactive males, preferred their own strain, and a similar preference was found in the inactive females. This beginning of a functional division between the two experimental populations illustrated evolution as a consequence of behavioural change by genetic manipulation. The two populations were used in a wide range of investigations in subsequent years.

In 1967, a long-standing collaboration in behaviour genetics was begun with Barrie Burnet of the Department of Genetics. Studies examined developmental and evolutionary problems, using single-gene mutants as a means of 'dissecting' behaviour. For example, the role of sounds produced by males during courtship was explored by introducing genes known to change specific components of the sensory system. Females carrying these genes were less responsive to male courtship song, and males with them were less successful in courtship, because their ability to use feedback to monitor the song output was impaired.

Kevin Connolly and Neville Moray also examined the imprinting of following responses in young chickens. This behaviour, first described by Lorenz in young geese, attracted much interest in the 1960s, because it suggested the existence of sensitive periods of development. Studies in the department examined the parameters involved in chickens' reactions to a simulated parent. Research issues included the duration of exposure, the intensity of stimulation, and the definition of a 'critical period' during which contact with the stimulus was essential for following to occur.

In the early 1960s, Neville Moray studied vision in an unusual plankton. Funded in part by the Royal Society, he worked for several periods at the Stazione Zoologica in Naples. With Richard Gregory from the University of Cambridge, he investigated the evolution of vision in what appeared to be a scanning eye with only one receptor.

Some publications during the decade were:

Burnet, B., Connolly, K. and Beck, J. Phenogenetic studies on visual acuity in Drosophila Melanogaster. Journal of Insect Physiology, 1968, 14, 855-860.

Connolly, K. J. Locomotor activity in Drosophila as a function of food deprivation. Nature, 1966, 209, 222.

Connolly, K. J. The social facilitation of preening behaviour in Drosophila Melanogaster. Animal Behaviour, 1968, 16, 385-391.

Connolly, K. J. Imprinting and the following response as a function of amount of training in domestic chicks. British Journal of Psychology, 1968, 59, 453-460.

Connolly, K. J., Burnet, B. and Sewell, D. Selective mating and eye pigmentation: An analysis of the visual component in the courtship behaviour of Drosophila Melanogaster. Evolution, 1969, 23, 548-559.

Connolly, K. J. and Moray, N.   The measurement of imprinting. Animal Behaviour, 1964, 12, 209-212.

Gregory, R. L., Moray, N. and Ross, H.   The curious eye of Copelia. Nature, 1965, 201, 1167-1168.

Kay, H. and Oldfield-Box, H.   A study of learning sets with an apparatus using three-dimensional shapes.   Animal Behaviour, 1965, 13, 19-24.

Kay, H. and Sime, M. E.   Discrimination learning with old and young rats. Journal of Gerontology, 1961, 17, 75-80.

Moray, N. and Connolly, K. J.   A possible case of the genetic assimilation of behaviour. Nature, 1963, 199, 358-360.

Oldfield-Box, H.   Social organization of rats in a 'social problem' situation. Nature, 1967, 213, 533-534.

Oldfield-Box, H. and Kay, H.   Four-choice visual discrimination tasks in the formation of learning sets by rats.   Animal Behaviour, 1963, 11 518-521.

Wright, P. L., Kay, H. and Sime, M. E.   The establishment of learning sets in rats.   Journal of Comparative and Physiological Psychology, 1963, 56, 200-203.

Developmental Psychology

Staff and graduate students working in this area in the 1960s included Rod Ashton, Sandy Cohen, Kevin Connolly, John Elliott, Rosemary Evison, Ann Harrison, Bill Jones, Norman Marsh, David Parsons, Helen Rosenberg, Peter Smith, Peter Stratton and Susan Stuart-Harris.

Kevin Connolly supervised research in three areas of developmental psychology: examining motor activities in handicapped and non-handicapped children of varying ages, studying variations in conditioning among new-born babies, and observing children's behaviour and social interaction in everyday situations.

The first set of studies was supported by the Spastics Society (now renamed Scope).   John Elliott, Bill Jones, Peter Stratton and Susan Stuart-Harris worked with Kevin to record and understand the development of children's motor skills.   For example, the speed and accuracy of performance in a serial assembly task was studied between the ages of 6 and 10, examining differences in grasp, movement and release.   Variables such as target size and amount of practice were manipulated, in part to provide baseline data for studies of cerebral palsied children.   'Associated' movements (accompanying an intended motor function but not necessary to it) are often found in children with brain damage, and those were also examined across the years from 4 to 16.

Other work in this field investigated the relationship between visual and kinaesthetic processing at different ages. Skills within a single sensory mode were found to be superior to cross-modal skills at all ages, but cross-modal interdependence became more important with increasing age. A model of the translation of information between modalities was developed.

Processes of operant conditioning were of particular interest. These were thought to have potential for teaching cerebral palsied children greater control of unwanted movements, on the basis that feedback signals to control their motor actions were affected by random noise. In order to help children to extract key information from movements made, processes of augmented feedback were developed.

Using the 'clown face operant apparatus' (known familiarly as 'Beppoe the clown', designed in conjunction with Max Sime), children had to move their arms rapidly and within (experimenter-adjusted) accuracy and time constraints, to hit the lighted nose of the clown face. Explicit feedback about performance was provided, and there was evidence that this procedure improved motor learning. Specific muscle movements were investigated by Ann Harrison, for example using techniques of electromyography.

In a second set of studies, Kevin Connolly, Rod Ashton and Peter Stratton investigated learning by new-born babies. Research funded by the Medical Research Council examined classical conditioning of head-movement and other reflexes in infants less than 90 hours old. Since obtaining responses to controlled stimuli from extremely young babies is difficult, a sound-proof chamber was constructed in the Jessop Maternity Hospital, and babies were placed there in cots for examination. Contemporary thinking was that learning was not possible before at least 15 days, but positive conditioning results showed that to be incorrect.

A third set of investigations, commencing in 1967, was influenced by ethological approaches to the observation on animals and people in everyday settings. Kevin Connolly and Peter Smith observed social interaction among pre-school children in nursery schools. Observational procedures were developed and standardised, providing a basis for projects in the 1970s which examined interaction at different ages in an experimental nursery school.

Some publications during the decade were:

Connolly, K. J. The applications of operant conditioning to the measurement and development on motor skill in children. Developmental Medicine and Child Neurology, 1968, 10, 697-705.

Connolly, K. J., Brown, K. and Bassett, E. Developmental changes in some components of a motor skill. British Journal of Psychology, 1968, 59, 305-314.

Connolly, K. J. and Stratton, P. Developmental changes in associated movements. Developmental Medicine and Child Neurology, 1968, 10, 49-56.

Connolly, K. J. and Stratton, P. An exploration of some parameters affecting classical conditioning in the neonate. Child Development, 1969, 40, 431-441.

Connolly, K. J. and Jones, B. A developmental study of afferent-reafferent integration. British Journal of Psychology, 1970, 61, 259-266.

Social Psychology

Staff and graduate students working in this area in the 1960s included Tom Coffman, Ian Croft, Steve Duck, Valerie Haycock, Christopher Knapper, Jerry Lovatt, Geoffrey Pilkington, Steve Simpson, Stuart Smith, Christopher Spencer and Peter Warr.

Social psychological studies in the department during the period were of three main kinds. First, measures to tap attitudes were developed and applied. For example, Geoffrey Pilkington and Pam Poppleton examined religious attitudes held by male and female university students. Patterns over time were explored. Peter Warr and colleagues examined the social orientations of ethnocentrism and authoritarianism. Ethnocentrism involves an exaggerated distinction between in-groups and out-groups, such that members of the latter (foreigners, young people, etc.) are strongly negatively evaluated. Authoritarianism was conventionally measured by an F-scale (for 'fascism'), and assessments were made in terms of attitudes to features such as family discipline, censorship, strong leadership, conventional behaviour, and the punishment of individuals who violate group standards.

Those attitudes were examined in terms of their structure as well as their content. Parallel research was from the perspective of cognitive complexity-simplicity, seeking to distinguish between more concrete and abstract thinking. Multidimensional scaling and other procedures were applied to judgements of several kinds to identify the number of dimensions likely to underlie them, for example seeking to find differences in cognitive differentiation between individuals with different personality, attitudes and other characteristics. Related studies examined correlates of the consistent tendency to make more extreme or less extreme judgements.

A second set of investigations explored aspects of person perception, supported by a research grant from the Nuffield Foundation (1963-1966). Peter Warr and Christopher Knapper were particularly interested in perceptions made through the medium of newspapers, radio or television (referred to as 'indirect perception'), and examined the influence on judgement of several features within those media. For example, variations in verbal and visual material were compared, and differences in judgement associated with different perceiver characteristics were explored.

Perceptions were recorded on 'semantic differential' scales (with response options between adjectives of opposite meaning), and methodological investigations into such scales were an important part of the project. An overall model of person perception was devised, and comparisons were drawn with processes of object perception. Subsequent work was funded by the Social Science Research Council (1967-1970), involving Tom Coffman and Stuart Smith, to specify perceptual decision rules in the judgement of other people and to undertake computer simulations of their operation.

Third, Chris Spencer focussed on what became known as 'social identity theory'. For example, he looked to see whether adolescents in secondary schools identified more with family of origin or anticipated social group. He also carried out experimental studies of decision making in groups, in particular to determine the effect of group discussions in polarising individual opinions.

Some publications during the decade were:

Pilkington, G. W. and Poppleton, P. K. The measurement of religious attitudes in a university population. British Journal of Social and Clinical Psychology, 1963, 2, 20-36.

Pilkington, G. W., Poppleton, P. K. and Robertshaw, G. Changes in religious attitudes and practices during university degree courses. British Journal of Educational Psychology, 1965, 35, 150-157.

Spencer, C. P., Ellis, H. D. and Box, H. O. Matched groups and the risky shift phenomenon. British Journal of Social and Clinical

Psychology, 1969, 8, 333-339.

Warr, P. B. and Coffman, T. L. Personality, involvement and extremity of judgement. British Journal of Social and Clinical Psychology, 1970, 9, 108-121.

Warr, P. B. and Knapper, C. K. The relative importance of verbal and visual information in indirect person perception. British Journal of Social and Clinical Psychology, 1966, 5, 118-127.

Warr, P. B. and Knapper, C. K. The Perception of People and Events. Chichester: Wiley, 1968.

Warr, P. B. and Smith, J. S. Combining information about people: Comparative tests between six models. Journal of Personality and Social Psychology, 1970, 16, 55-65.

Warr, P. B., Schroder, H. M. and Blackman, S. The structure of political judgment. British Journal of Social and Clinical Psychology, 1969, 8, 32-43.

Abnormal and Clinical Psychology

Staff and graduate students working in this area in the 1960s included Kenneth Garwood, Peter McKellar, Daniel McKerracher, Alan McKinnon, Ian Murphy and Don Rossi.

All of those except Peter McKellar undertook PhD projects under Peter's supervision, mostly associated with clinical psychologist roles at Rampton Special Hospital. Topics included stress and aggression, factors associated with fear, and the psychological characteristics of murderers and rapists.

Peter McKellar himself was particularly interested in variations in mental imagery and the factors associated with those variations. He investigated imagery in specific groups, such as police officers and anatomists, and the ways in which different kinds of images were used in their jobs. He also studied emotions such as anger, and their manifestations in potentially criminal behaviour. Time estimation was examined as a function of personality, current context, and physiological conditions such as oxygen lack.

Prior to the appointment of John Davis in 1969, the department had no clinically-trained staff. John Orme, a local NHS clinical psychologist, contributed to departmental teaching (see Chapter 4), and in his early years in Sheffield he too undertook PhD research supervised by Peter McKellar. John examined the estimates of time made by different groups of clinical patients (with anxiety, depression, schizophrenia, etc.), and compared those with time estimates made by non-patients.

Some publications during the decade were:

Connolly, K. J. and McKellar, T. P. H. Forensic psychology. <u>Bulletin of the British Psychological Society</u>, 1963, 16, 1-8.

McKellar, T. P. H. The investigation of mental images. In S. A. Barnett and A. McLaren (eds.), <u>Penguin Science Survey 1965</u>. London: Penguin, 1965.

McKellar, T. P. H. <u>Experience and Behaviour</u>. London: Penguin, 1968.

Orme, J. E. <u>Time Experience and Behaviour</u>. London: Iliffe, 1967.

Occupational Psychology

Staff and graduate students working in this area in the 1960s included John Annett, Michael Bird, Bernard Dodd, Harry Kay, Neil Rackham, Max Sime and Peter Warr.

The department's occupational research included studies summarised below into programmed instruction and through the MRC Social and Applied Psychology Unit. Other occupational work, described in this section, was of two main kinds: studies with local steel firms to understand and assist technological change, and investigations into management learning.

As part of a project funded by the Department of Scientific and Industrial Research (1961-1963), John Annett and Max Sime worked in a local steel company that was moving from open-hearth steel furnaces to electric-arc furnaces. In order to develop effective training in that area, it was important to understand the nature of skills involved in both jobs. Procedures were developed and applied of hierarchical task analysis, and studies were made of the new training procedures. Bernard Dodd later developed this project with funding from the Science Research Council, to examine individual differences in learning and in the effective introduction of change.

In the middle of the decade (1964-1966), funds were received from the British Iron and Steel Federation to examine the role of supervisors in the steel industry, with particular emphasis on skill requirements and training needs. Peter Warr and Michael Bird distributed questionnaires to all supervisors in the locality and interviewed a representative sample of those, to identify factors associated with training participation and success. Recommendations were implemented and evaluated in local steel companies.

This concern for effective training was later extended through a research grant from the Ministry of Labour (1966-1969) to examine in-company schemes for the development of managers. Peter Warr, Michael Bird and Neil Rackham created and applied procedures in several steel and airline companies to measure the outcomes of training immediately after it had finished and later in the work situation. Factors influencing those learning and transfer outcomes, as well as trainees' reactions to a programme, were identified and measured, and a general model of training evaluation was developed.

Some publications during the decade were:

Bird, M. W. Changes in work behaviour following supervisory training. Journal of Management Studies, 1969, 6, 331-345.

Dodd, B. T. A study in adult retraining: The gas man. Occupational Psychology, 1967, 41, 143-153.

Warr, P. B. and Bird, M. W. Identifying Supervisory Training Needs. London: Her Majesty's Stationery Office, 1968. (Training Information Paper 2.)

Warr, P. B., Bird, M. W. and Rackham, N. H. Evaluation of Management Training. London: Gower Press, 1970.

Warr, P. B. and Routledge, T. An opinion scale for the study of managers' job satisfaction. Journal of Occupational Psychology, 1969, 43, 95-109.

Studies of Teaching Machines and Programmed Instruction

Staff and graduate students working in this area in the 1960s included John Beck, Graham Boyce, Bernard Dodd, James Hartley, Henry Hudson, Harry Kay, Christopher Knapper, Bill Laidlaw, Sheila Marston, David Moore, Max Sime, Gordon Stock, Peter Warr and Quentin Whitlock.

Associated with investigations of learning in the laboratory and of training in companies (see above), the department was a national leader in studies of what were sometimes called 'auto-instructional methods'. Interest in teaching machines and programmed instruction expanded rapidly in the early 1960s, and the department's research successes and provision of practical advice gave rise to a high reputation in business, educational and government settings. Grants were received from the Department of Scientific and Industrial

Research (1960-1963), the Science Research Council (1963-1967), the Ministry of Defence (1967-1969) and the Ministry of Labour (1967-1971). The last of those funded a new Programmed Instruction Centre for Industry.

Key principles of structured learning were explored, and those were embodied in devices to present information, control student activities and record performance. Those devices took the form of 'teaching machines' or 'programmed texts'. In the latter case, students were required to answer a question after reading material on each page of a book; they were then directed through other pages, not necessarily consecutively[82]. In the former case, equivalent material was presented through table-top equipment created from metal and plastic.

Teaching machines or programmed texts exhibited a large number of 'frames' in either a 'linear' manner (a single route for all learners) or in a 'branching' mode (where a person's route was determined by previous performance). Information was provided in each frame, and a student had to answer a question posed (usually but not always by making a selection from multiple options). The linear programmes proceeded in small increments, with theoretical justification in B. F. Skinner's model of 'shaping' behaviour. The branching programmes posed questions to which answers were more likely to be incorrect, and thus likely to require remedial action.

Members of the department tried out several approaches (for example, in teaching statistics and physiological psychology for its own students), and developed the 'Sheffield teaching machine', in which material was stored on film and presented on a rear-projection screen. A student responded to each frame's question by writing an answer on a card and posting that into a chute on the front of the machine[83]. That action led to presentation of the correct answer, and the student next pressed a key to indicate whether his or her answer had been correct. Remedial frames were activated in the case of an incorrect answer.

Creating machines of this kind was technically troublesome and extremely time-consuming; separate components had to be designed, created and integrated within a purpose-built metal frame. In addition, teaching programmes had to be written after detailed task analysis and the specification of criterion attainments. One Sheffield development was of a group teaching machine, with material for all learners

---

[82] The contents were spelled as 'programmes', rather than as in the later preference for computer 'programs'.

[83] Some other early machines required learners to write answers on a roll of continuous paper, which was then advanced by turning a knob.

presented from a single slide-projector and each student responding through his or her multi-choice response box.

Ideas and practical procedures of this kind were of great interest in the 1960s, and the department received a large number of requests for information and advice. Research applications were undertaken in many companies and government bodies. Some studies used commercially-produced machines or their text-based equivalent, comparing different forms of programme against each other or against human teachers. Several programmes written by staff were subsequently produced by commercial publishers, and the royalties received were placed in a fund to support additional research in the department.

This work was undertaken in an era before computers were available for interaction with users in real-time; almost all computer use was for off-line data-manipulation. By the end of the decade, it was clear that the arduous technical development and associated hardware limitations of teaching machines could be bypassed by computer-based procedures. The general principles of learning, emphasising the specification of criterion performance, structuring of material and the adaptation of teaching input to individual progress, came to be applied in more general perspectives.

Thus, when the Programmed Instruction Centre for Industry was set up in the department in 1967, the concern was with effective training in general despite a principal focus on programmed learning. With Harry Kay as Director and Bernard Dodd as Research Director, the centre was funded by the Ministry of Labour (later renamed the Department of Employment and Productivity). It had three aims: to provide information about research findings and good practice, to give advice and assist in validation studies, and to carry out new research studies. For example, surveys of company training procedures were carried out, methods of task analysis were developed, and comparative studies of different training inputs were made. A key aim was the development and better understanding of 'self-correcting systems', which operated by obtaining and using relevant feedback about recent performance.

Also in 1967, Harry Kay and Max Sime obtained a research grant from the Ministry of Defence, to examine issues in programmed instruction in class-room settings. Employing Graham Boyce, this work compared presentation and other factors in learning with the Sheffield group teaching machine (see above), for example in army settings where map-reading or technical procedures were being learned.

Consistent with a general move toward computer applications, the project also included exploration of computer-based teaching in military training schools.

The department's work in this field was mainly directed at adult, rather than child, learners. Parallel studies were carried out in the university's Department of Education, where Ken Austwick developed programmed learning applications in mathematics for school-children. He received grants from the Ministry of Education and elsewhere for this work. Links with the Department of Psychology were sustained by Harry Kay's supervision of Ken's PhD research.

Some publications during the decade were:

Dodd, B. T. A diagnostic branching system for remedial training in the manipulation of vulgar fractions. Programmed Learning and Educational Technology, 1967, 4, 28-37.

Hartley, J. Some problems of internal and external evaluation of programmes. Programmed Instruction, 1963, 3, 5-6.

Kay, H., Annett, J. and Sime, M. E. Teaching Machines and Their Use in Industry. London: Her Majesty's Stationery Office, 1963. (Problems of Progress in Industry 14.)

Kay, H., Dodd, B. and Sime, M. Teaching Machines and Programmed Instruction. London: Penguin, 1968.

Sime, M. E. Computers as test beds for teaching systems. Journal of the Association for Programmed Learning, 1968, 5, 53-65.

Sime, M. E. and Boyce, G. C. Overt responses, knowledge of results and learning. Journal of the Association for Programmed Learning, 1969, 6, 12-19.

The Development of Computers in Psychological Research

Staff and graduate students working in this area in the 1960s included Mike Fitter, Thomas Green, Godfrey Harrison, Harry Kay, Neville Moray and Max Sime.

At the beginning of the decade, computers were employed almost entirely for off-line calculations. Within universities it was usual for a 'mainframe' to be located centrally, and employed for administrative as well as research purposes. No psychology department in Britain had its own computer.

The potential for on-line psychological work (in 'real time') was much discussed in the Sheffield department from about 1963. However, it was not clear from where funds might be obtained, since a request to a research council would not be for a specific project and it would be entirely novel. In 1965 a bid was made by Harry Kay and Neville Moray to the Psychology Committee of the Science Research Council, for the purchase and development of an Elliott 903C computer.

The proposal spelled out two main reasons for the project. First was the need for "a small on-line computer to monitor and analyse experiments, particularly in the study of learning processes". Current studies were said to have reached the stage where building special equipment was uneconomical and ineffective. Second was a more general need "to study how the behavioural sciences may best use computers for on-line experiments"; "in this country we have been surprisingly slow to develop studies of this kind".

It was proposed to create computer-assisted training devices, in which the nature of stimuli presented would be contingent on preceding responses. Other studies would examine recall and recognition, problem-solving, reaction times and physiological responses. The computer would be used to generate, present, record and analyse material. "It is desirable that the decision logic be supplied by a small computer with the following units: an arithmetic unit for addition, subtraction, multiplication and division; a core store of several thousand words for programmes (sic) and data; a flexible input-output system for special peripherals, teleprinter and paper tape input-output".

The application was successful, and the 903C was installed in November 1966. Sheffield became the first British psychology department to acquire such a facility. The machine (from Elliott-Automation Computers Limited) included a central processor with 8192 word core store (for 18-bit words), a paper-tape reader and a punch, and an analogue input unit for the attachment of experimental equipment as designed. Also provided was a 'kit of components for constructing special-purpose equipment'[84]. The machine was about two metres wide, one metre deep and one metre high; it was sited at floor level. A photograph is on page 97.

Commissioning and customising the computer took many months. The system had previously been used mainly in military applications, and no interfaces for laboratory use were available. Max Sime, Neville Moray and technician Lionel Hinbest worked long hours on hardware development, and Thomas Green wrote and integrated

---

[84] Practical difficulties at the time were illustrated in a record on the installation document that a carton of teleprinter paper could not be delivered because of a general shortage.

many necessary programs, including a COWSEL compiler to permit LISP-like programming. The system became increasingly used across the department's research programme.

The operation of the 903 required cumbersome preparations, including checking and winding up substantial lengths of paper tape (of different colours, coded according to content)[85] and correctly setting approximately 30 switches. Tape-handling skills had to be acquired, for mending broken lengths with adhesive tape and punching replacement holes over the joined area with a special piece of equipment. More substantially, staff and graduate students also had to acquire programming skills (using ALGOL or BASIC languages), aided in part by Thomas Green's written guides. Teaching about programming and interface design was provided in the Graduate School (see Chapter 4). For many early studies, new input-output devices had to be created, although later investigations could of course make use of previously-built equipment.

In conjunction with work to create programs for use in the department, Thomas Green initiated research into the usability of different forms of computer language. Experimental comparisons were made between linguistic properties that might reduce errors and increase the ease with which a language is learned.

Linked to its concern to develop knowledge about computers and psychology more generally, the department applied to the NATO Science Committee for funds to hold an Advanced Study Institute on On-Line Computing for Psychology. This took place in Sheffield in July 1969, bringing together 59 psychologists from Europe and North America to review procedures available at the time. In addition to discussions about current issues and possible ways forward, papers were presented by Ward Edwards, Douglas Creelman, Max Sime, M. M. Taylor and D. M. Forsyth, J. G. F. Francis and N. S. Sutherland, George Sperling, Neville Moray, and Donald Norman.

Many publications in this area appeared in the 1970s, by which time the system was fully operational. One output during the previous decade was: Moray, N. <u>On-line Computing for Psychology: Proceedings of a NATO ASI</u>. Sheffield: Department of Psychology, 1969.

---

[85] The master tapes, needed for all uses, were maintained primarily by Adrian Simpson.

The MRC Social and Applied Psychology Unit

Staff of the unit in the 1960s included Richard Crabtree, George Hespe, Harry Kay, Alan Little, Max Sime and Peter Warr.

In 1964, the Medical Research Council (MRC) set up a Committee on Research in Industrial and Applied Psychology[86]. This examined current provision in the country and explored future research needs and possibilities. It concluded (in 1967) that "there is a serious lack of research in the field of applied and industrial research" and recommended the establishment of a new unit to help remedy that deficit. Harry Kay was asked to submit proposals for such a unit. Those were accepted by MRC, and a new research centre opened within the Department of Psychology in October 1968. It became known as the MRC Social and Applied Psychology Unit. Harry Kay was initially the Honorary Director, and Peter Warr was Assistant Director.

Proposals for the unit were drawn up in conjunction with Max Sime and Peter Warr, and were based in part on their research interests. The unit's general theme was identified as 'applied cognitive studies', and research was to be carried out both in employing organisations and in the laboratory. Occupational psychology at the time was largely atheoretical and concerned with one-off descriptive case studies of particular problems and solutions. The unit's programme differed from much other work by addressing practical issues from an explicitly academic standpoint.

It was planned to carry out computer-based studies by extending the department's Elliott 903C, but the Medical Research Council preferred to purchase a new machine from Computer Technology Ltd. This was a Modular One, which operated rapidly for its time and had a modular architecture allowing different configurations to be selected for different purposes. Despite those advantages and a relatively large memory, this computer lacked software for experimental work, and substantial initial programming was needed before it could be used in psychological research. It was not commissioned in the unit until 1970.

The unit's Terms of Reference were agreed in 1968 as follows:

1. Examination of complex judgements and decision-making in practical industrial situations with particular emphasis in the laboratory investigations upon the use of on-line computer facilities.

2. Development of models of decision-making and pursuit of their

---

[86] Harry Kay was one member of that committee.

practical applications through a manager-computer system.

3. Study of actual decision-making procedures in order to identify strategies and styles; incorporation of these into a manager-computer system for development within the unit.

4. Development of practical understanding of other, related forms of judgement.

5. Examination of the nature of risk-taking, perception of fairness in economic and social confrontations, and judgements about productivity: studies, implications and practical relevance.

6. Development of a general model of complex judgement with application to judgements of people, of social and industrial events and to decision-making.

Initial projects built upon previous work in the department, for instance examining the content and structure of judgements about people and events. Studies of employee participation were initiated in several organisations, and research set out to measure and better understand work motivation among managers. Investigations into computer-assisted decision-making became possible once the Modular One was operational.

The subsequent development of the Social and Applied Psychology Unit has been described by Warr (1999). It came to focus on employee well-being and effectiveness, and received funds also from the Economic and Social Research Council and other bodies. It remained active in the Sheffield department until 1996.

6. REFERENCES

Anon (1922). Professor Green. Floreamus![87], 10, 75, 203-204.

Ballard, P. B. (1910). Handwork as an Educational Medium. London: Allen and Unwin.

Bartlett, F. C. (1949). What is industrial psychology? Occupational Psychology, 23, 212-218.

Benjamin, L. T. (2000). The psychology laboratory at the turn of the 20th century. American Psychologist, 55, 318-321.

Birchenough, C. (1911). The psychological bases of school geography. Journal of Experimental Pedagogy, 1, 45-51, 128-136.

Blackstone, T. (1980). Student unrest in the '60s: Some reflections. In E. Fearn and B. Simon (eds.), Education in the Nineteen Sixties. London: History of Education Society.

Boring, E. G. (1929, 1950). A History of Experimental Psychology. New York: Appleton-Century-Crofts.

Broadbent, D. E. (1970). Sir Frederic Bartlett: An appreciation. Bulletin of the British Psychological Society, 23, 1-3.

Bunn, G. C., Lovie, A. D. and Richards, G. D. (eds.) (2001). Psychology in Britain: Historical Essays and Personal Recollections. Leicester: British Psychological Society.

Chapman, A. W. (1955). The Story of a Modern University: A History of the University of Sheffield. Oxford: Oxford University Press.

Edgell, B. (1947). The British Psychological Society. British Journal of Psychology, 37, 113-132.

Esper, E. E. (1964). A History of Psychology. Philadelphia: Saunders.

Fink, C., Gassert, P. and Junker, D. (eds.) (1998). 1968, the World Transformed. Cambridge: Cambridge University Press.

Flugel, J. C. (1933, 1951, 1964). A Hundred Years of Psychology. London: Duckworth.

Flugel, J. C. (1954). A hundred years or so of psychology at University College London. Bulletin of the British Psychological Society, 27, 21-31.

---

[87] Floreamus!, founded in 1897, described itself as 'a Chronicle of University College, Sheffield'. When the College was granted a Royal Charter in 1905, the description became 'a Chronicle of the University of Sheffield'. It recorded significant events, and in its earlier years included 'effusions of literary aspirants'. Publication continued until 1928, when it was replaced by the student magazine Arrows.

Gill, E. J. (1912a). Methods of teaching reading: A comparison of results. Journal of Experimental Pedagogy, 1, 243-248.

Gill, E. J. (1912b). The teaching of spelling. Journal of Experimental Pedagogy, 1, 310-319.

Green, J. A. (1910). The University of Sheffield. In W. S. Porter and A. T. Watson (eds.), British Association Handbook and Guide to Sheffield, pp.135-152. Sheffield: Northend.

Green, J. A. (1920). Normal performance of teachers. Journal of Experimental Pedagogy, 5, 245-248.

Gretton, J. (1969). Students and Workers: An Analytical Account of Dissent in France, May-June 1968. London: Macdonald.

Hearnshaw, L. S. (1962). Sixty years of psychology. Bulletin of the British Psychological Society, 46, 2-10.

Hearnshaw, L. S. (1964). A Short History of British Psychology 1840-1940. London: Methuen

Holdstock, L. (1998). The ratio of male to female undergraduates. In J. Radford (ed.), Gender and Choice in Education and Occupation, pp. 59-83. London: Routledge.

Holdstock, L. and Radford, J. (1998). Psychology passes its 1997 exams. The Psychologist, 11(3), 117-119.

Johnston, K. L. (1911a). M. Binet's method for the measurement of intelligence – Some results. Journal of Experimental Pedagogy, 1, 24-31.

Johnston, K. L. (1911b). The measurement of intelligence: Binet-Simon tests. Journal of Experimental Pedagogy, 1, 148-157.

Kay, H. (1960). The Psychologist's Task. Sheffield: University of Sheffield.

Kay, H. (1996). A long innings. In J. D. Mollon (ed.), The Experimental Psychology Society 1946-1996, pp. 15-16. Cambridge: Experimental Psychology Society.

Knight, R. (1962). The Department of Psychology in the University of Aberdeen. Bulletin of the British Psychological Society, 47, 3-11.

Layard, R., King, J. and Moser, C. (1969). The Impact of Robbins. London: Penguin.

Lovie, A. D. (1998). The BPS and 2001: Centenary? What centenary? Current Trends in History and Philosophy of Psychology, 2, 1-8.

Marwick, A. (1998). The Sixties: Cultural Revolution in Britain, France, Italy, and the United States, c.1958-c.1974. Oxford: Oxford University Press.

Mollon, J. D. (ed.) (1996). The Experimental Psychology Society 1946-1996. Cambridge: Experimental Psychology Society.

References

Morrell, J. (1997). Science at Oxford 1914-1939: Transforming an Arts University. Oxford: Clarendon Press.

Murphy, G. (1928, 1929, 1932, 1938, 1949). Historical Introduction to Modern Psychology. London: Kegan Paul.

Myers, C. S. (1936) Autobiography. In C. A. Murchison (ed.), A History of Psychology in Autobiography, volume 3, pp. 215-230. Worcester, Massachusetts: Clark University Press. Reprinted in Occupational Psychology, 1970, 44, 5-13.

Neve, H. (1997). Dr Fred Esher: Founder of the North of England Branch. The Psychologist, 10, 21-22.

Oldfield, R. C. (1950). Psychology in Oxford -- 1898-1949. Bulletin of the British Psychological Society, 9, 345-353, and 10, 382-387.

Pear, T. H. (1955). The Manchester University Department of Psychology 1909-1951. Bulletin of the British Psychological Society, 26, 21-30.

Robbins, Lord. (1963). Report on Higher Education. London: Her Majesty's Stationery Office.

Rooke, M. A. (1971). Anarchy and Apathy: Student Unrest 1968-70. London: Hamish Hamilton,

Russell, R. W. and Summerfield, A. (1956). British psychologists, their training and placement, 1949-1951. Bulletin of the British Psychological Society, 28, 29-50.

Shimmin, S. and Wallis, D. (1994). Fifty Years of Occupational Psychology in Britain. Leicester: British Psychological Society.

Smith, P. K., Ashton, R. S., Elliott, J. M, Freeland, C., Jones, W. D., McKinnon, A. A., Simpson, S. J. C. and Strong, R. J. (1969). Sixth-formers and psychology: A survey. Bulletin of the British Psychological Society, 22, 205-212.

Sutherland, G. (1984). Ability, Merit and Measurement: Mental Testing and English Education 1880-1940. Oxford: Clarendon Press.

Taylor, N. G. R. (1916). Further data towards the study of the Binet-Simon scale. Journal of Experimental Pedagogy, 3, 256-266.

Thomas, J. B. (1982). J. A. Green, educational psychology and the Journal of Experimental Pedagogy. History of Education Society Bulletin, 41-45.

Valentine, E. (1997). Psychology at Bedford College London 1849-1985. London: Royal Holloway.

Valentine, E . (1998). Psychology at Bedford College London 1849-1985. Current Trends in History and Philosophy of Psychology, 1, 1-7.

Valentine, E . R. (1999). The founding of the psychological laboratory, University College London: "Dear Galton . . . Yours truly, J. Sully". History of Psychology, 2, 204-218.

Ward, H. (1922). John Alfred Green. Journal of Experimental Pedagogy, 6, 261-263.

Warr, P. B. (1999). Work, Well-being and Effectiveness: A History of the MRC/ESRC Social and Applied Psychology Unit. Sheffield: Sheffield Academic Press.

Wooldridge, A. (1994). Measuring the Mind: Education and Psychology in England, c.1860-c.1990. Cambridge: Cambridge University Press.

Two Heads of Department

John Alfred Green, Professor of Education 1906-1922

Harry Kay, Professor of Psychology 1960-1972

Some Staff in the 1960s

John Beck

Mike Bird

Graham Boyce

Tom Coffman

Jack Clarkson

Kevin Connolly

Valerie Haycock

John Frisby

Jerry Lovatt

David Marks

Peter McKellar

Geoff Pilkington

Neil Rackham

Adrian Simpson

Peter Smith

David Slater

Chris Spencer

Peter Warr

The Mushroom Lane Building in 1968

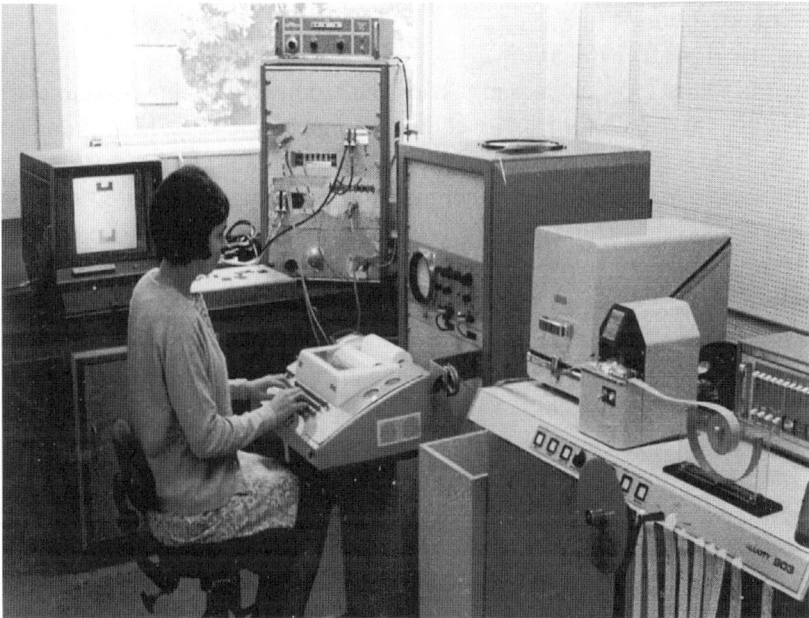

The Elliott 903 Computer with Experimental Peripherals

APPENDIX 1: MEMBERS OF THE PSYCHOLOGY DEPARTMENT TO 1970

This appendix describes members of the Sheffield Psychology Department up to the end of the academic year 1969-1970[88]. Additional information about each person has been presented in earlier chapters.

Most of those listed have contributed information towards the summaries below. People identified as 'graduate students' worked towards their PhD degree during the period, and 'research staff' were funded by external institutions on specific, time-limited projects. Members of 'teaching staff' were employed by the University of Sheffield, for three years as an Assistant Lecturer and otherwise on an open-ended contract.

In addition to members of those three groups, administrative and technical staff in the period included Vera Amor, Jean Beal, Mick Cruse, Margaret Dobson, Bill Dyson, Eric Eagle, Sylvia Gadsby, Alice Gavins, Kathy Gregory, Lionel Hinbest, Mary Jessop, Diane Kirkup, Toni Rossi, Susan McCarthy, Christine Mitchell, Barbara Taylor and Paul Williams.

Annett, John
Research staff, 1960-1963.

Since 1955, John had carried out studies of human learning with Harry Kay in Oxford. He continued that work in a new project in Sheffield, funded by the Department of Scientific and Industrial Research, to extend theoretical principles to create automated methods of instruction. The Sheffield project developed and evaluated several forms of programmed instruction, in both laboratory and industrial settings. Parallel studies with funds from the US Navy examined feedback in auditory discrimination tasks. John also served as an Honorary Lecturer, presenting statistics in the department partly through teaching machines or programmed texts.

He moved to a Lectureship at the University of Aberdeen in 1963, and to a Readership at Hull University in 1965. He became a Professor in the Open University in 1972 and at the University of Warwick in 1974. He retired in 1995, continuing as a Professor Emeritus.

---

[88] Also included are Charles Baker, Adrian Gilbert and Pam Poppleton, who were employed as psychologists in the Department of Philosophy.

Arnold, Paul
Research staff, 1962-1965.

A graduate in Zoology, Paul worked as a Research Assistant with Neville Moray, examining genetic assimilation in the department's colony of drosophila melanogaster. He subsequently took a degree in psychology at the University of Nottingham, followed by a PhD. He became a Lecturer in Psychology at the University of Manchester, where his later research interests concerned cognitive and social aspects of deafness.

Ashton, Rod
Graduate student, 1967-1970.

Rod's PhD work was funded by the Medical Research Council and supervised by Kevin Connolly, examining variations in states of alertness in new-born babies. In 1970, he moved to a Lectureship in Psychology at the University of Lagos, and two years later he took up a similar position at the University of Queensland, Brisbane, Australia. He was Head of that department between 1980 and 1987. His interests have covered areas of biophysiology, imagery and the lateralisation of cognitive functions.

Baggaley, Jon
Graduate student, 1968-1971.

Jon's PhD research concerned the psychology of music, examining sensations of colour associated with pitch perception. He also started work with Steve Duck on psychological aspects of communication processes, and this collaboration has continued ever since.

Jon was a Lecturer in Communication Studies at Liverpool University between 1971 and 1979, in which year he became an Associate Professor in the Memorial University of Newfoundland, Canada. Between 1983 and 1994, he was Associate Professor and Professor in the Department of Education in Concordia University, Montreal, and from 1996 he has been Professor and Director of Educational Technology in Athabasca University, Alberta. He has a special interest in the educational effects of communications media.

Baker, Charles
Research staff, 1957-1960.

Charles joined the Psychological Laboratory in the Department of Philosophy in 1957, initiating the Behavioural Research Unit with funds from the British Iron and Steel Research Association and later the Flying Personnel Research Committee. He examined human factors issues in industrial settings, and taught statistics, research methods and occupational psychology.

Charles moved to a Lectureship in Psychology at the University of Durham at the end of 1960, where he developed business research and consultancy with colleagues from other disciplines. He was influential in the creation of Durham University Business School in 1967, became a Professor of Management in 1975, was Director of the Business School until 1984, and retired in 1993.

Beck, John
Research staff, 1967-1969.

John carried out research within the Programmed Instruction Centre for Industry, undertaking surveys and practical studies in several organisations. He subsequently taught in the Department of Extramural Studies, at Sheffield Polytechnic and in the University of Manchester Institute of Science and Technology. In 1984, he joined the National University of Singapore, later moving to the City Polytechnic of Hong Kong. He returned to Singapore to become an Associate Professor at Nanyang Business School in 1992. His recent research interests have been in management development and cross-cultural training.

Bird, Michael
Research staff, 1964-1969.

Michael joined the department after research into animal behaviour at Durham University and a post-graduate degree in ergonomics at Loughborough University. He worked with Peter Warr, first on studies of supervisors in the iron and steel industry (1964-1966, funded by the British Iron and Steel Federation) and then (also with Neil Rackham) on the evaluation of management training (funded by the Ministry of Labour, later renamed the Department of Employment and Productivity).

On completion of those projects, he moved to Ashorne Hill College, the management training centre for the British steel industry. This became part of the British Steel Corporation and later of British Steel plc. Mike worked as a Director of Studies, and retired in 1995.

Box, Hilary
Research staff, 1961-1967.

After graduating in psychology and philosophy at the University of Bristol, Hilary moved to Sheffield to work with Harry Kay on an MRC grant to examine mammalian ageing. The focus was on the acquisition of learning sets in younger and older rodents. Between 1963 and 1967, she was funded by the University of Sheffield to study social behaviour and learning in rodents, looking particularly at the division of labour among rats learning in groups. She also assisted with teaching, presenting animal laboratory classes and lecturing in aspects of social psychology.

In 1967, Hilary moved to a Lectureship in Psychology at the University of Reading. She established a course in animal behaviour, and set up an animal laboratory with a range of species. A joint degree in psychology and zoology was established in the early 1970s. She became a Senior Lecturer in 1993. Her research has mainly concerned marmoset monkeys, with a particular focus on their social behaviour and social learning. She is a past president of the Primate Society of Great Britain and has been vice-president of the International Primatological Society.

Boyce, Graham
Research staff, 1967-1969.

Graham worked with Max Sime in testing applications of programmed learning. Financed by a grant from the Ministry of Defence, he studied the impact of variations in the pacing and content of teaching in military and university settings.

Bradshaw, John
Graduate student, 1964-1967.

John's PhD work was funded by the Science Research Council, and concerned pupil size as a measure of arousal during problem-solving. While at Sheffield, he also organised summer vacation Land Rover trips into North Africa, on which he was joined by other graduate students. He moved to the University of Otago as a Lecturer in Psychology (1967-1968), and has since been at Monash University, Australia, as a Lecturer, Senior Lecturer and Professor. His main research interests have been in experimental neuropsychology, skilled performance and attention, and the evolution of language.

Clarkson, Jack
Research staff, 1962-1964. Teaching staff, 1964-1974.

Jack joined the department from Oxford University and a period at Stanford University, USA, to work on the role of feedback in auditory discrimination tasks. Directed by John Annett, this project was funded by the US Navy. He also undertook statistics teaching and provided advice about statistical issues to staff as well as students. He was appointed an Honorary Lecturer in 1963 and a Lecturer in 1964.

Jack moved to the University of Otago, New Zealand, in 1974, as a Senior Lecturer in Psychology. He taught statistics and contributed to student and staff projects in many areas of the discipline. He retired in 1987.

Coffman, Tom
Research staff, 1967-1969.

Tom joined the department after completing his PhD on social stereotyping in Princeton University, USA. He worked with Peter Warr and Stuart Smith on a project funded by the Social Science Research Council to develop computer simulations of person perception. He returned to USA in 1969, holding several academic appointments in Virginia Polytechnic, Duke University and Roanoke College. Subsequently he founded a company locating and selling second-hand books.

Cohen, Sandy
Graduate student, 1966-1973.

Sandy moved from Kent State University, USA, to undertake PhD research into children's learning. From 1969, he worked with Kevin Connolly and Norman Marsh to investigate the application of operant conditioning and augmented feedback to motor skill development in brain-damaged children, funded by the Spastics Society (since renamed Scope).

He returned to Ohio in 1973, to work in the family business, and from 1978 pursued a career as photographer and computer animator. In 1980, he founded a company to apply his interests in synaesthesia and the neurophysiology of visual and auditory perception, developing ways to integrate computer graphics and computer music. Since 1985, he has undertaken that work from Berkeley, California, using computers to combine visual experiences with the aural sensations of music.

Connolly, Kevin
Research staff, 1961-1962. Teaching staff, 1965-1999.

Kevin joined the department in 1961 to work with Neville Moray on a project in behaviour genetics supported by a grant from the

Medical Research Council. In 1962, he was appointed an Assistant Lecturer in Psychology at Birkbeck College, University of London, and a Lecturer in 1963. In 1965, he returned to Sheffield as a Lecturer with responsibility for teaching comparative and developmental psychology, becoming a Senior Lecturer in 1969 and Professor in 1971. He was Head of Department between 1972 and 1980 and between 1983 and 1986, becoming a Professor Emeritus in 1999.

Kevin was chairman of the Scientific Affairs Board of the British Psychological Society between 1976 and 1979, and President of the Society 1980-1981. In 1969, he received the Society's Spearman Medal for published research of outstanding merit. He has served as chairman of the Association of Child Psychology and Psychiatry and as President of Section J (Psychology) of the British Association for the Advancement of Science.

In comparative psychology, his research interests have centred on the genetics and evolution of behaviour, often working with Dr Barrie Burnet of the Sheffield Department of Genetics. Research in developmental psychology has explored issues such as the behaviour of new-borns, play and social interaction in pre-schoolers, motor development, particularly hand function, and the effects of iodine deficiency on foetal development. This last work was carried out on a pre-literate population in the Western Highlands of New Guinea.

Cook, Robert
Graduate student, 1968-1971. Research staff, 1971-1972.

Robert's PhD research was supervised by Kevin Connolly, into the genetics of courtship behaviour in fruit flies. Subsequent to his Medical Research Council studentship, he remained in the department as a post-doctoral researcher for a further year.

Between 1972 and 1982, Robert held research fellowships at the Laboratoire de Génétique des Populations, Montpellier, France, Latrobe University, Melbourne, Australia, and the Max-Planck Institute for Biological Cybernetics, Tübingen, Germany. He then founded a software company in South East Australia, creating programs for accountancy and other businesses; in addition, he grows and sell grapes for wine-making.

Crabtree, Richard
Research staff, 1969-1973.

Richard was previously employed in the Computing Department of Nottingham University. He joined the MRC Social and Applied

Psychology Unit to assist in work to use the Modular One computer in studies of industrial decision-making. This involved the development of software and the establishment of an experimental laboratory in which individuals interacted in problem-solving tasks with the computer. Task requirements were based on processes of decision-making in a local steel plant, using information and criteria from that setting.

In 1973, Richard moved to the British Steel Corporation, contributing to computer systems development. He subsequently worked in similar roles as an independent consultant and (since 1983) for Barclays Bank.

Croft, Ian
Graduate student, 1968-1971.

Ian carried out research into person perception, supervised by Peter Warr. In 1971, he became an Assistant Lecturer in the Psychology Department at the University of Newcastle on Tyne. Since promoted to a Lecturer in that department, his research interests have primarily concerned group processes and personal construct theory.

Davies, Ian
Graduate student, 1968-1971.

Ian worked on visual cognition, examining parallel and serial processing of shape features. He moved as a Lecturer to the Department of Psychology at the new University of Surrey in 1971, subsequently becoming a Senior Lecturer, Reader and (in 1996) Professor. He became Head of that department in 1999. Ian's research interests have been mainly in the perception of medical images, the perception of spatial layout in displays, categorical perception, and the influence of language on colour perception.

Davis, John
Teaching staff, 1969-1977.

Following degrees in mathematics and in philosophy, psychology, and physiology, John studied and worked in clinical psychology in USA between 1962 and 1967. After a year teaching at the Oxford College of Technology (now Oxford Brookes University), he joined the Sheffield department as a Lecturer with responsibility for clinical psychology. His early research interests centred on behaviour in clinical interviews and on aspects of self-disclosure.

John left Sheffield in 1977, to become a Senior Lecturer at the

University of Warwick. In addition to other teaching in clinical psychology, he established a degree course in psychotherapy for clinical psychologists. He was active in studies of dissociative disorders and of the international development of clinical psychology. He retired from his university post in 1997, and continued clinical work with the National Health Service.

Dodd, Bernard
Research staff, 1962-1971.

After obtaining an MA in psychology from the University of Aberdeen, Bernard joined the department to work with Harry Kay (financed by the Department of Scientific and Industrial Research and later the Science Research Council) on the development of training procedures in industrial settings, particularly through self-instructional materials. Additional funding was obtained in 1967 from the Ministry of Labour (later renamed the Department of Employment and Productivity) to establish a Programmed Instruction Centre for Industry, of which Bernard became Research Director. The centre provided advice and information about applications in occupational settings and carried out problem-solving research in organisations.

In 1971, Bernard moved to Inbucon Learning Systems as a consultant on training and selection. He subsequently became Head of Training Research in the Admiralty Research Laboratory and later Head of Selection for naval ratings. He retired in 1990.

Duck, Steve
Graduate student, 1968-1971.

Steve was funded by the Social Science Research Council for PhD research into personal construct theory and the formation of friendships and group cohesiveness, supervised by Chris Spencer. In 1981, he moved to a Lectureship in Social Psychology at the University of Glasgow, and between 1973 and 1986 was at the University of Lancaster as a Lecturer and Senior Lecturer. He became a Research Professor at the University of Iowa, USA, in 1986, later becoming Chair of the Department of Communication Studies and Adjunct Professor of Psychology.

Steve has retained an interest in the processes of relationship formation and decline, founding the Journal of Personal Relationships and the International Network on Personal Relationships. He has focussed particularly on everyday communication in the context of personal relationships.

Dudley, Bob
Graduate student, 1966-1968.

Bob worked on individual differences in vigilance in prolonged-attention tasks, supervised by Adrian Simpson.

Elliott, John
Research staff, 1967-1971. Teaching staff, 1971-1973 and 1976-1986.

John succeeded Hilary Oldfield-Box in supervising the department's colony of rats, and used those (as a Part-time Demonstrator) in providing instruction about maze behaviour. His own research, supervised by Kevin Connolly, concerned ethological studies of hand function in young children and (later, funded by the Spastics Society) investigations into children's visual discrimination of orientation.

He left in 1973 to serve as a psychologist to the Ministry of Social Affairs in Singapore, but was re-appointed as a Lecturer in the Sheffield department in 1976. He returned to Singapore ten years later as a Senior Lecturer in the National University of Singapore's new degree programme in psychology, where his interests expanded into memory functioning, parent-child relations, and aspects of occupational psychology.

Evison, Rosemary
Graduate student, 1965-1967.

Prior to moving into psychology, Rose had been employed as a teacher. After graduating in the department, she worked with Kevin Connolly on research into perceptual and motor skills deficits of children with disabilities. She next became a Lecturer and then a Research Fellow in Colleges of Education in Doncaster and Leeds respectively.

She subsequently moved into the field of organisational development, creating (with Neil Rackham) procedures of behaviour analysis for application to interpersonal processes. She extended that interest into co-counselling and to devise cognitive-emotional counselling procedures. She has worked for several years as a consultant and trainer in change strategies. Recent projects have focussed on the management of emotions in organisations.

Fitter, Mike
Research staff, 1968-1971 and 1974-1992.

A graduate in physics and mathematics, Mike joined the

department as a research assistant to Neville Moray, on a three-year grant from the Science Research Council. This examined the division of attention and the selection of information in psychophysical tasks, testing contemporary theories of selective attention. On Neville's departure in 1970, the work continued in conjunction with Adrian Simpson.

Mike moved to a Lectureship at Birkbeck College, London, in 1971, but returned to the MRC Social and Applied Psychology Unit in 1974. He worked initially on studies of computers and decision-making, developing that research to examine psychological aspects of medical computing. He left the unit in 1992, becoming a self-employed consultant to health-care and other organisations.

Freeland, Carol
Graduate student, 1967-1969.

Frisby, John
Graduate student, 1965-1968. Teaching staff, 1968-present.

John's first work in the department was PhD research on oriented channels for visual motion perception, supervised by Neville Moray. He became an Assistant Lecturer in 1968, a Lecturer in 1969, and a Professor in 1976. He was Head of Department between 1980 and 1983 and again between 1991 and 2000. In conjunction with John Mayhew he founded the Artificial Intelligence Vision Research Unit in the department in 1984. He was responsible with Rod Nicolson for introducing the university's degree in Cognitive Science in 1990.

John's research and teaching interests have blended computational and psychophysiological approaches to cognitive science, with particular emphasis on vision. In an interdisciplinary field that typically requires key contributions from mathematicians, his contribution has been to use psychophysics to ask whether a given method is implemented in human vision. His main research topic has been stereoscopic vision, and he has devised a test of stereovision that is in standard use worldwide.

Garwood, Kenneth
Part-time graduate student, 1958-1961.

Kenneth was employed as a psychologist in Rampton Special Hospital. Associated with Peter McKellar's interest in forensic psychology, they worked together on studies with patients in the hospital. His PhD thesis was entitled 'A psychological study of human fear'.

Gilbert, Adrian
Teaching staff, 1948-1955.

Adrian was the first person appointed in the Department of Philosophy to provide teaching in psychology as part of the university's General Degree. He was previously employed by the Industrial Health Research Board of the Medical Research Council.

Green, Thomas
Research staff, 1965-1984.

Thomas joined the department from the Experimental Programming Unit in the University of Edinburgh. He was initially employed as a researcher funded by IBM, on a project supervised by Neville Moray to examine the role of syntactic cues in sentence perception. He then worked with Harry Kay and Max Sime on a Science Research Council project to examine choice-response time and errors. He was also active in developing the department's computer system, writing programs and providing guidance to colleagues in use of that system.

In 1970, Thomas joined the MRC Social and Applied Psychology Unit, investigating the role of computers in decision-making and the design of programming languages. He transferred to the MRC Applied Psychology Unit in Cambridge in 1984, from which he retired in 1996. He then became an Honorary Research Fellow at the Computer-Based Learning Unit at the University of Leeds.

Harrison, Ann
Graduate student, 1968-1971. Research staff, 1971-1978.

Ann's PhD research, supervised by Kevin Connolly, examined limb movements in children with cerebral palsy. Using electromyography, she developed feedback procedures to improve motor control and sensory monitoring. She continued this work as a Research Assistant, financed by the National Fund for Research into Crippling Diseases.

In 1978, she joined the Department of Community Medicine and Behavioral Sciences at the new School of Medicine in Kuwait, where she carried out research into pain and community provisions for disabled people. After a period at the United Arab Emirates University (1991-1996), she joined St George's University in Grenada, West Indies, where she has been a Professor and Dean of the School of Arts and Sciences. She moved to Virginia, USA, in 2001.

Harrison, Godfrey
Graduate student, 1962-1964. Research staff, 1964-1968.

Godfrey carried out PhD research into retention strategies in short-term memory, and from 1964 was funded through an SSRC grant awarded to Harry Kay and Neville Moray. He was active in the installation and development of the department's Elliott 903C computer.

Godfrey was appointed a Lecturer in Psychology at the University of Hull in 1968, and later became a Lecturer and Senior Lecturer at University College Cardiff. In 1983, he moved to the National University of Singapore's English Language and Literature Department to pursue interests in bilingualism and language development. Three years later, with John Elliott, he initiated that university's degree course in psychology. Between 1989 and 1996 he worked in the University of Hong Kong's Department of Speech and Hearing Sciences.

Hartley, James
Graduate student, 1961-1964.

Jim was supervised by Harry Kay in PhD studies of programmed learning, comparing the effectiveness of linear and branching programs in the teaching of logarithms. He then took up an appointment as Assistant Lecturer in the Psychology Department at the University of Keele, later becoming a Lecturer, Senior Lecturer, Reader and Professor. He was head of that department between 1982 and 1992. In 1970-1971, he taught at Memorial University in St John's, Newfoundland, and in 1977-1978 he worked at Bell Telephone Laboratories in New Jersey, USA.

Jim's research interests have included programmed instruction, typography and layout, teaching and learning in higher education, and computer-aided writing. He retired from teaching in 1997, becoming an Honorary Research Professor at Keele.

Haycock, Valerie
Graduate student, 1966-1969.
See Stewart, Valerie.

Hespe, George
Research staff, 1968-1973.

George joined the MRC Social and Applied Psychology Unit from a position in industrial management, and worked on studies of employee participation. He subsequently became a Lecturer in the university's School of Management.

Horrell, Ian
Graduate student, 1964-1968.

Ian carried out research into geometric illusions, examining those as possible examples of inappropriate visual constancy scaling, being supervised by Neville Moray. He also served as a temporary Assistant Lecturer in 1967 and 1968. In the latter year he moved to the University of Hull as a Lecturer in Psychology, becoming a Senior Lecturer in 1988.

Ian has carried out research into neurophysiological systems underlying reinforcement processes, and has interests in the application of behavioural sciences to farming.

Howe, Michael
Graduate student, 1963-1966.

Mike carried out PhD research into recall and storage in human memory, supervised by Harry Kay. He then became a Post-doctoral Fellow at Dalhousie University, Canada (1966-1967), an Assistant Professor of Education in Tufts University, USA (1967-1969), and an Associate Professor of Educational Psychology in the University of Alberta, Canada (1969-1971).

Mike moved to the Department of Psychology in the University of Exeter in 1971, where he has been a Lecturer, Senior Lecturer, Reader and (since 1991) Professor. His research activities have covered human memory, learning, and high abilities. Studies have examined the early backgrounds of exceptionally competent young musicians, and factors influencing the creativity and achievement of individuals in general.

Hudson, Henry
Research staff, 1969-1973.

Henry joined the Programmed Instruction Centre for Industry after a career in the Royal Air Force. He became Deputy Director of the centre in 1972, and moved to Sheffield Polytechnic[89] in 1973, to

---

[89] Sheffield Polytechnic became Sheffield Hallam University in 1992.

direct the Learning Resources Unit. That unit provided advice to public and private organisations about effective learning procedures.

Jones, Bill
Graduate student, 1967-1970.

Bill's PhD research, supervised by Kevin Connolly, concerned cross-modal perception in children, and examined blind as well as normally-sighted individuals. He was a Lecturer in Psychology at the University of Queensland, Australia, between 1971 and 1975, with a visiting appointment at the University of Waterloo, Canada, in 1973 and 1974. In 1975, he moved to the Department of Psychology at Carleton University, Ottawa, Canada, being Chairperson from 1986 to 1997.

Bill's research interests gradually moved away from experimental psychology, becoming more concerned with psychological issues in organisational functioning.

Jordan, Ann
Graduate student, 1965-1967.

Ann carried out studies in conjunction with Neville Moray into aspects of short-term memory. She left in 1967, to accompany her husband to his new job in Canada.

Kay, Harry
Teaching staff, 1960-1972.

Military service in world war two interrupted Harry's degree studies at the University of Cambridge. He obtained an MA degree in 1947, and was subsequently employed in the Nuffield Research Unit for Ageing at that university, where he studied age patterns in adult learning. He became a Lecturer in Experimental Psychology at the University of Oxford in 1951, undertaking research into aspects of skills and learning. He moved to Sheffield as head of the new Psychology Department in January 1960.

During the 1950s and 1960s, Harry held many positions in addition to his university role. For example, he served as a council member of the British Psychological Society, the British Association for the Advancement of Science, the Social Science Research Council and the National Institute for Industrial Psychology. He was President of the Experimental Psychology Society, and a member of the Civil Service Selection Board, the Psychology Committee of the Social Science Research Council, a number of Medical Research Council and

Science Research Council committees, and several working parties of the University Grants Commission and of the Department of Scientific and Industrial Research. He was President of the British Psychological Society in 1971-1972.

Harry's teaching in Sheffield mainly concerned experimental psychology, and he supervised several research programmes (see Chapter 5). He was also active in wider university roles, for example in creating the Academic Development Committee in 1963 (becoming its first Chairman) and being appointed a Pro Vice-Chancellor in 1967. He moved to the University of Exeter in 1972 in the position of Vice-Chancellor, retiring in 1989.

Knapper, Christopher
Research staff, 1962-1966.

Following a period in the cutlery industry, Chris was appointed to a research position in the department's project to examine applications of programmed instruction. Funded by the Department of Scientific and Industrial Research, and supervised by Harry Kay and John Annett, the project designed and assessed different types of teaching programmes. From 1963, he worked with Peter Warr on a project financed by the Nuffield Foundation to examine factors influencing how newspaper communications are perceived.

At the end of that grant, Chris became an Instructor in Psychology at the University of Saskatchewan, Canada. He was promoted to Associate Professor and Professor there in 1969 and 1976. He later joined the University of Waterloo as Professor of Psychology and founding Director of the Teaching Resource Office, before moving to Queen's University in Kingston, Ontario, as Professor of Psychology and of Education and as Director of a new Instructional Development Center. His interests have been primarily in teaching and learning in higher education.

Laidlaw, Bill
Research staff, 1969-1971.

Bill was employed as Information Officer in the Programmed Instruction Centre for Industry, funded by the Department of Employment and Productivity.

Little, Alan
Research staff, 1968-1970.

Graduating in the department in 1968, Alan joined the MRC

Social and Applied Psychology Unit on its foundation, to work with George Hespe on studies of employee participation. He moved to a position in management consultancy, and pursued a career in that field.

Lovatt, Jerry
Graduate student, 1966-1969.

Jerry's PhD research was funded by the Social Science Research Council and supervised by Peter Warr. It developed and tested mathematical models of impression formation in laboratory settings. He then became a market research executive with the Schlackman Research Organisation, subsequently being promoted to Joint Managing Director. Between 1977 and 1988, he held marketing and strategic planning positions with Reynolds Tobacco, Del Monte Foods, and Nabisco International. Since 1988, he has had his own consultancy firm, working primarily in continental Europe and the Far East.

Marks, David
Graduate student, 1966-1969.

David's PhD work, supervised by Jack Clarkson, examined subjective probability judgements,. On its completion, he took up a position as Lecturer in Psychology at the University of Otago, New Zealand, to which Peter McKellar had moved in the previous year. He became a Senior Lecturer in 1974. In 1986, he returned to the United Kingdom as Head of the School of Psychology at Middlesex Polytechnic (now University). He became Head of their Health Research Centre in 1989, and in 2000 he moved to City University as Director of the Health and Counselling Psychology Research Centre.

David's research interests have concerned mental imagery, consciousness, health psychology and health promotion. Specific projects have included cognitive therapy for smokers, studies of dementia care, and the evaluation of health promotion programmes.

Marsh, Norman
Research staff, 1969-1974.

Norman joined the department on a five-year contract funded by the Spastics Society (since renamed Scope) at the beginning of 1969. His background was in electronic instrumentation and control engineering, and he worked to develop mathematical models of skilled performance. He also contributed programs and documentation for the Department's Elliott 903C computer.

On completion of the grant, Norman took an MSc course in

statistics at the University of Leeds, and was in 1975 appointed to an academic post in the Department of Psychology at the University of Liverpool. He retired from that Department in 1997.

Marston, Sheila
Research staff, 1968-1971.

Sheila worked in the Programmed Instruction Centre for Industry, developing and testing procedures for nurse training (for instance, in kidney dialysis). She then moved to Sheffield Polytechnic, working in the Learning Resources Centre.

McKellar, Peter
Teaching staff, 1955-1968.

Peter graduated in psychology from the University of Otago, New Zealand. After obtaining a PhD in London and holding the post of Lecturer at the University of Aberdeen, he was appointed a Lecturer in Psychology in the Sheffield Department of Philosophy. He was promoted to Senior Lecturer in 1958, moving into the new Department of Psychology in 1960. He spent the academic year 1963-1964 as Visiting Professor in the Highlands University of New Mexico, USA, and in 1968 moved as Professor and Head of the Psychology Department to the University of Otago, New Zealand. After retirement, he returned to the United Kingdom.

Peter's teaching at Sheffield initially covered most areas of psychology, but after the appointment of additional staff he concentrated on personality and abnormal psychology. He also contributed to external teaching, for example to medical students, police officers, magistrates and evening class students. His research interests in the 1960s covered imagery, thinking, emotions and remembering.

McKerracher, Daniel
Graduate student, 1965-1968.

Daniel's PhD research was supervised by Peter McKellar, examining factors influencing the stability of sub-normal and psychopathic patients. He moved to Canada, and later became Professor of Education at the University of Otago in New Zealand.

McKinnon, Alan
Graduate student, 1967-1970.

Al came to the department from Saskatchewan, Canada, to

undertake PhD research into sensory deprivation supervised by Peter McKellar. After Peter's departure in 1968, Al's interests extended into the effect of stress on mental states.

Moore, David
Graduate student, 1963-1966.

David was funded by a PhD studentship from the J. Arthur Rank Foundation, to develop group applications of teaching machines, supervised by Harry Kay. He then worked for a year as a teacher, before (in 1968) taking a position in Memorial University of Newfoundland to develop off-campus television courses for teachers in remote areas. In 1972, David became a clinical psychologist in the Isle of Man, later becoming a member of the island's parliament. After taking on financial responsibilities in that role, he worked in senior positions with several insurance companies.

Moray, Neville
Teaching staff, 1960-1970.

Neville became a Lecturer in the department after a period as Assistant Lecturer in the University of Hull. He was promoted to Senior Lecturer in 1966, spent the academic year 1967-1968 as Visiting Associate Professor in the Massachusetts Institute of Technology, and in 1970 was appointed Associate Professor in the University of Toronto, Canada. He was subsequently employed at the Universities of Stirling, Illinois (USA), Valenciennes (France) and Surrey.

Neville's teaching responsibilities at Sheffield covered physiological and comparative psychology, and he presented laboratory practical classes. His principal research interests at the time were in selective auditory attention and behaviour genetics, and he examined related issues in collaboration with colleagues and students: synthesised speech, divided attention, auditory short-term memory, imprinting in chickens and vision in plankton. Subsequent interests have included the design of human-machine systems, the integration of psychology and engineering, and human factors in nuclear safety.

Murphy, Ian
Graduate student, 1958-1961.

Ian was funded by the Medical Research Council for PhD research into stress reactivity in aggressive offenders. He was jointly supervised by Peter McKellar and John Tong, staff psychologist at Rampton Special Hospital. In 1961, Ian was appointed a clinical psychologist in Sheffield, and worked in therapeutic roles with several types of patient. More recently, he specialised in procedures for children with difficulties, and was a Consultant Psychologist in Child and Adolescent Psychiatry. He retired in 1997.

Newsome, Rex
Research staff, 1965-1966.

Rex spent a year in the department as a Leverhulme Fellow, following PhD research at the University of Queensland, Australia, into perceptual processes in driver behaviour. He subsequently worked at the Road Research Laboratory in Berkshire, before returning to a Lectureship, and subsequently a Senior Lectureship, at the University of Queensland. He remained there until his retirement in 1996.

His research and teaching interests concerned human factors aspects of road safety and psychological issues in the rehabilitation of disabled people. He served on many local and national committees in Australia working for people with disabilities.

Oldfield-Box, Hilary
Research staff, 1961-1967.
See Box, Hilary.

Parsons, David
Part-time graduate student, 1966-1972.

David enrolled as a part-time PhD student whilst working as a research assistant in the university's Department of Child Health. In that role he assessed the intellectual development of children with hydrocephalus and spina bifida, and his own research focussed on the verbal behaviour of the children studied. In 1972, he joined the Department of Employment's Industrial Rehabilitation Unit in Sheffield, from which he retired in 1992. He has since worked as a consultant.

Pilkington, Geoffrey
Teaching staff, 1955-1983.

Geoffrey was appointed Assistant Lecturer in 1955, and promoted to Lecturer and Senior Lecturer in 1958 and 1967 respectively. He was responsible for one of the two lecture courses and all practical classes for students in their Intermediate (first) year. He took early voluntary retirement in 1983.

Geoffrey was particularly interested in epistemological issues, such as psychology's legitimacy to be considered a natural science, and whether the subject requires its own method of inquiry such as introspection. He carried out empirical studies into the measurement of religious attitudes, and examined the pattern of those across the years of university education.

Poppleton, Pam
Research staff, 1959-1960.

Pam joined the department on a two-year contract financed by the Ministry of Defence. Supervised by Peter McKellar and Charles Baker, the research examined perceptual problems in map-reading. She also undertook teaching in social psychology.

In 1960, on the departure of Reg Edwards from the Department of Education, Pam was appointed a Lecturer in his place. For some years, she continued teaching Social Psychology in the Psychology Department and worked with Geoffrey Pilkington on studies of religious attitudes. She was subsequently promoted to Senior Lecturer and served as head of the Division of Education between 1982 and 1985. She retired in 1985, and later contributed to an international study of the working lives of secondary school teachers.

Rackham, Neil
Research staff, 1966-1969.

Neil worked with Peter Warr and Mike Bird on the evaluation of management training, funded by the Ministry of Labour, later renamed the Department of Employment and Productivity. As part of that work, he developed and applied procedures to record interpersonal interaction in, for instance, meetings of managers before and after training.

At the end of his contract, he set up a company (Huthwaite Consultants) to develop applications of those procedures, particularly in selling and negotiation interactions. He later moved to the United States, becoming Chairman of Huthwaite Inc., and publishing several books about psychological and organisational issues.

Roberts (previously Stuart-Harris), Susan
Research staff, 1967-1968.

Susan worked as a Research Assistant with Kevin Connolly on a programme funded by the Spastics Society (since renamed Scope) to examine the development of motor skills in children. She studied information processing between the ages of six and ten, identifying factors that influence the speed and accuracy of motor responses. She left in 1968, with the aim of becoming an educational psychologist. That involved two years teaching in a Sheffield first school, followed by a postgraduate course at University College, London, between 1970 and 1971.

Susan joined the Essex Educational Psychology service in 1971, becoming Area Senior Educational Psychologist in 1975. After several years employed part-time, while caring for her family, she returned to full-time work in 1988, becoming an Area Senior again in 1998.

Rosenberg, Helen
Research staff, 1968-1970.

Helen worked as a Research Assistant with Kevin Connolly and Norman Marsh on a programme funded by the Spastics Society (now Scope). She examined information-processing strategies in motor skill learning by disabled and normally developing children.

Rossi, Don
Graduate student, 1965-1967. Teaching staff, 1967-1968.

Don joined the department as a PhD student after MSc studies in the University of New Mexico in USA. Supervised by Peter McKellar, he carried out research into the characteristics of individuals convicted of murder or rape (in Rampton Special Hospital). He also contributed to teaching in social psychology and psychometric testing, and joined Peter McKellar in presenting forensic psychology to local police officers.

In 1968, he moved to Baltimore, USA, as a clinical psychology intern. He then gained a fellowship for training as a child and adult psycho-analyst, and joined the staff of the University of Michigan Medical School. He subsequently became Director of the Behavioral Science Department of the Michigan State Police, where he developed a programme to meet the mental health needs of police officers and their families. Other activities included hostage negotiation, critical incident management and support for criminal investigations. Don subsequently established a private clinical practice which is now in Holt, Michigan.

Salter, David
Graduate student, 1965-1969. Teaching staff, 1969-1971.

David was initially a PhD student, supervised by Neville Moray, investigating selective attention and perception after delayed speech feedback. In 1969 he was appointed a temporary Assistant Lecturer, teaching experimental aspects of the subject. He moved to a Lectureship at the University of Newcastle upon Tyne in 1971 and retired in 1997.

Sewell, David
Graduate student, 1969-1972.

David carried out PhD research in behaviour genetics, funded by the Medical Research Council, and supervised by Kevin Connolly and Barrie Burnet (Department of Genetics). He next became an Assistant Lecturer in Psychology at the University of Hull, and has since been Head of that department and Dean of the Faculty of Science and the Environment. His research interests have remained in behaviour genetics, but also extend to neuropsychology, information technology and exercise psychology.

Sime, Max
Research staff, 1960-1984.

Max joined the department from Oxford with Harry Kay in 1960. He had worked with Harry on research into psychological aspects of ageing funded by the Medical Research Council, and in Sheffield was financed by the Department of Scientific and Industrial Research until 1963, the Science Research Council until 1966, and the Social Science Research Council until 1968. In that last year he became one of the founding members of the new MRC Social and Applied Psychology Unit.

Max's initial work in Sheffield was with Harry Kay, John Annett and Peter Warr on the development of teaching machines, for which he created apparatus and carried out experimental comparisons. He was active in the installation and development of the Department's Elliott 903C computer (from 1966), which provided a flexible basis for laboratory experimentation and was widely used by colleagues. In the Social and Applied Psychology Unit, he became responsible for research into computer applications to decision-making, working with Thomas Green and others. He retired in 1984.

Simpson, Adrian
Teaching staff, 1966-1995.

Adrian joined the department as an Assistant Lecturer in 1966, from PhD work into signal detection theory at the University of Reading. He became a Lecturer in 1968. His research and teaching were primarily in areas of cognitive-experimental psychology and in statistics. Studies in the former area examined processes of attention (in collaboration with the Department of Mechanical Engineering), language, and cerebral laterality. In the latter area, Adrian developed methods to improve teaching, sometimes in conjunction with other departments of the university

His interest in statistics led him to apply quantitative methods in fields such as primate behaviour and (in collaboration with the Speech Science Department) developmental language disorders. He retired in 1995, but remained active in the department, continuing to teach statistics to undergraduate and graduate groups.

Simpson, Steve
Graduate student, 1967-1968.

Steve joined the department to investigate processes of person perception, leaving after a year.

Smith, Peter
Graduate student, 1967-1970. Research staff, 1971-1974. Teaching staff, 1974-1995.

Peter's PhD research was funded by a Nuffield Biological Scholarship (one year) and a Medical Research Council Studentship (two years). Supervised by Kevin Connolly, he carried out naturalistic studies of children's social and play behaviour in day nurseries. Subsequent to his PhD, he worked with Kevin on a project funded by the Social Science Research Council, examining how social and environmental factors affected the behaviour of pre-school children. In 1974, he was appointed a Lecturer in the department, becoming a Senior Lecturer in 1983, a Reader in 1985, and Head of Department between 1986 and 1989. He was awarded a Personal Chair in 1991.

During those years, Peter carried out investigations into children's play and into bullying in schools. In 1995, he became a Professor in the Psychology Department of Goldsmiths College in the University of London. His research interests have continued to focus on bullying among children, and have also included grandparenting and evolutionary approaches to human behaviour.

Smith, Stuart
Research staff, 1967-1970.

Stuart worked with Peter Warr and Tom Coffman on a project funded by the Social Science Research Council to develop computer simulations of person perception. He then moved to the Department of

Management Studies in Sheffield City Polytechnic (which became Sheffield Hallam University in 1992), where up to 1987 he was successively a Lecturer, Senior Lecturer and Principal Lecturer. Between 1988 and 1997, Stuart was Professor of Change Management in Sheffield Business School, and since that date he has worked independently as an organisation and management development consultant.

Spencer, Christopher
Teaching staff, 1968-present.

Chris joined the department as Assistant Lecturer in 1968 from a temporary Lectureship in the University of Reading. His DPhil work at Oxford had concerned sub-cultural differences in values and norms. He was promoted to Lecturer, Senior Lecturer and Reader in 1970, 1988 and 1992 respectively, and was Head of Department between 1989 and 1993. He was initially responsible for teaching social psychology, and carried out research into group decision-making and patterns of friendship. He established a lecture course in environmental psychology in 1970, and turned his research attention to children's understanding and use of places, blind people's way-finding and children's needs in city environments.

Chris took leave of absence between 1973 and 1974, to assist in the establishment of the Science University of Malaysia and its Social Science School, at that time developing collaborative research into primate behaviour and investigations into drug abuse; work of the latter kind was also carried out in Iran.

Stewart (previously Haycock), Valerie
Graduate student, 1966-1969.

Valerie carried out PhD studies into impression formation by children of different ages, supervised by Peter Warr. She next took up a teaching position at the University of Denver, USA, before working for IBM for a year. She has since been a consultant industrial psychologist, identifying and developing management talent and assisting in organisational change. Valerie has also developed practical applications of repertory grid procedures, and written several books about management and organisational development.

Stock, Gordon
Research staff, 1964-1965.

Gordon, previously a training officer in Samuel Fox and

Company, was seconded to the department for a year through the British Iron and Steel Federation, to evaluate and develop programmed instruction methods for the industry. He created a programme about the care and maintenance of bearings, which was subsequently used widely in several industries.

On return to his company, he led work to develop new personnel systems, and later became responsible for management development for a group of steel companies. In 1976, he became manager in charge of training and management development in Stocksbridge and Tinsley Park Works of the British Steel Corporation, from which he retired when the company was denationalised.

Stratton, Peter
Graduate student, 1965-1968. Research staff, 1968-1970.

Peter's PhD research, supervised by Kevin Connolly and funded by the Medical Research Council, examined classical conditioning of heart-rate responses in the human new-born, demonstrating substantial learning at very young ages. This work was continued through a two-year MRC award after completion of his studentship.

In 1970, Peter took up a Lectureship in Psychology at Leeds University, and extended the research into naturalistic adaptations in early childhood. He has since investigated aspects of child abuse and processes in families. In 1979 (with clinical psychologists) he founded the Leeds Family Therapy and Research Centre, which provides training and support in a research context. He is currently Director of that centre and a Senior Lecturer in the Psychology Department. In addition, he is Managing Director of The Psychology Business, a company that develops approaches from family and clinical research into industrial and commercial application.

Stretch, Roger
Graduate student, 1957-1960.

Roger carried out PhD research on the activity and exploratory behaviour of rats, supervised by Peter McKellar. The focus was on operant conditioning and its consequences. He also had a part-time teaching appointment, and worked with Charles Baker to assist local businesses in staff selection. Following the award of his degree Roger moved to the United States.

Strong, Richard
Graduate student, 1967-1970.

After studies of cognitive processes in Sheffield, Richard moved into positions in the scientific civil service. He was recently employed as a Principal Psychologist in the Centre for Human Sciences of the Defence Evaluation and Research Agency.

Stuart-Harris, Susan
Research staff, 1967-1968.
See Roberts, Susan.

Underwood, Geoffrey
Graduate student, 1969-1972.

Geoffrey was supervised by Neville Moray (to 1970) and then by Harry Kay, in PhD studies of selective attention to spoken language, using procedures of dichotic listening. The work was financed by the Science Research Council. He moved to a lecturing position in the University of Nottingham in 1972, and subsequently held posts in Canada at the University of Waterloo and the University of Guelph. He is currently Professor of Cognitive Psychology and Head of the School of Psychology at Nottingham.

Since leaving Sheffield, Geoffrey's research has continued to focus on the experimental study of attention, recently involving eye-movement investigations of readers, musicians and drivers. A general theme is the relationship between skill acquisition and changes in the distribution of visual attention.

Warr, Peter
Research staff, 1961-1962. Teaching staff, 1962-1968. Research staff, 1968-1996. Teaching staff, 1996-present.

Peter joined the department from a position in industry to work with Harry Kay, John Annett and Max Sime on aspects of programmed instruction. He also undertook PhD research into repetition and learning. He was appointed Assistant Lecturer and Lecturer in Social Psychology in 1962 and 1964, before becoming Assistant Director of the newly formed MRC Social and Applied Psychology Unit in 1968. He spent the year 1966-1967 as a Fulbright Scholar at Princeton University, USA.

Peter became Deputy Director of the Social and Applied Psychology Unit in 1971 and Director in 1973 after the departure of the Honorary Director, Harry Kay. He remained an Honorary Lecturer in the department, and became a Professor Associate in 1978. He received all three awards of the British Psychological Society for outstanding contributions to the development of the discipline: the Spearman Medal (1969), the Presidents' Award (1982) and an Honorary Fellowship (1997). He has been editor of the Journal of Occupational and Organizational Psychology and associate editor of several other journals. Work with government bodies has included membership of ERSC Council and of other ESRC and MRC committees. Since 1996, Peter has held a Personal Chair in the department.

His primary research activities in the 1960s concerned aspects of learning, interpersonal perception and the effectiveness of training. Later research has continued in those fields, as well as examining psychological well-being, associations between personality and behaviour, mental health during unemployment, age differences in cognition and in other processes, perceptions of oneself and of others, and the development of measuring instruments for studies in those areas.

Whelan, Ed
Graduate student, 1964-1967.

Ed's PhD research concerned visual perception and cerebral dominance. It was funded by the Medical Research Council and supervised by Neville Moray and Jack Clarkson. He next took a two-year MSc course in clinical psychology at Leeds University, and then moved to the Hester Adrian Research Centre at the University of Manchester, where he was a Lecturer (1969-1977) and a Senior Lecturer (to 1985). After two years as a Senior Lecturer in the Department of Education at the University of Manchester, he became a consultant clinical psychologist in Rochdale, with special responsibility for neuropsychology and physical handicap. He has worked in many parts of the world to develop procedures for vocational guidance and the rehabilitation for individuals with physical disabilities or learning difficulties.

Whitlock, Quentin
Research staff, 1969-1972.

Quentin was Information Officer in the Programmed Instruction Centre for Industry. He moved into a similar role in Sheffield Polytechnic, and in 1982 joined a business consultancy specialising in learning technology, computer-based training and multi-media systems.

Wright, Peter
Research staff, 1960-1961.

Peter worked with Harry Kay and Max Sime on a Medical Research Council project transferred from Oxford, examining how learning sets become established in rats. He was an investigator in the Social Science Research Centre of the University of Edinburgh between 1961 and 1964, studying the employment in Britain of immigrants from the commonwealth. He was then employed as an operational research scientist for a management consultancy (two years) and scientist developing personnel systems for Unilever (five years). In 1971 he became a Lecturer in Occupational Psychology at the University of Bradford Management Centre, where his main research interests concerned leadership and interpersonal skills.

APPENDIX 2: SOME EXAMINATION PAPERS FROM THE 1950s

A. Intermediate BA, 1954 (Four subjects were studied in Year One.)
B. Intermediate BA, 1959 (Four subjects were studied in Year One.)
C. General BA, 1954 (Three subjects were studied for a General degree.)
D. General BA, 1959 (Three subjects were studied for a General degree.)
E. Single Subject Honours BA Psychology, 1959

A. INTERMEDIATE PSYCHOLOGY EXAMINATION FOR THE DEGREE OF BA, 1954

PAPER I (Three hours) *Answer FIVE questions.*
1.   State McDougall's definition of an instinct and distinguish instinctive from reflex action. 2.   Define what is meant by receptor organ and show how different receptors have been classified. 3.   What are the social inductive processes? 4.   Examine the contention that the Mendelian laws of inheritance are too simple to account for the genetic transmission of psychological characteristics. 5.   State and discuss the psychological principles said to underly the spread of rumour in a social group. 6. Interpret the following formula and indicate how and in what circumstances you would apply it. *[The formula for correlation rho was presented here.]* 7. Write a short description of the principal parts and functions of the human brain. Draw diagrams wherever possible. 8. What is meant by social attitude? Describe some of the attempts made to measure social attitudes. 9. Discuss the relationship between the expressions of the emotions and the autonomic nervous system. 10. Write short notes on *four* of the following: (1) sex-linked character; (2) sociometry; (3) reaction time; (4) cretinism; (5) drive; (6) stereotype.
PAPER II (Three hours) *Attempt TWO tasks.*
1. Using the product moment formula, estimate the correlation between your subject's preferences and your own for the given material. 2. By applying the limiting method, or some variant of it, ascertain the two-point threshold for the tips of all four fingers of the left hand. 3. Ascertain an estimate of the errors, irrespective of sign, made by your subject in bisecting a line 10 cm. long. From a sample of 50 cases, calculate the mean and standard deviation. 4.   Using a simple

substitution task, design and execute an experiment to compare the two learning curves obtained from massed and distributed practice.

B. INTERMEDIATE PSYCHOLOGY EXAMINATION FOR THE DEGREE OF BA, 1959

PAPER I (Three hours) *Answer FOUR questions, THREE from Part A, and ONE AND ONE ONLY from Part B. Candidates are advised to make reference to their laboratory work wherever appropriate.*

PART A   1.   Indicate what you consider to be the principal contributions of Gestalt psychology to the understanding of perception. 2.   Indicate what is meant by "suggestion" and discuss the factors favourable to suggestibility.   3.   "You cannot change human nature." Discuss this statement in the light of your knowledge of the psychology of learning. 4.   Explain what are meant by "folkways" and discuss their influence upon social conformity.   5.   "One of the most obvious characteristics of perception is its selective nature." (MORGAN). Discuss. 6.   Analyse the process of learning into its main components and illustrate your analysis from experiments you have conducted.   7. Examine the factors which favour retention in human remembering.

PART B *Mathematical tables are available for use in this part of the examination.*

8.   Elucidate the concept of "statistical significance", showing its importance in interpreting the results of some experiments in psychology. 9.   Matched groups of 324 smokers and 225 non-smokers respectively were given a lecture on the relationship between smoking and lung cancer.   A month later a recall test for the contents of the lecture gave the following results. *[A table of mean items recalled and standard deviations for the two groups was presented here.]* Is there a statistically significant difference in recall as between smokers and non-smokers?

PAPER II (Three hours) *Answer FOUR questions of which AT LEAST ONE AND NOT MORE THAN TWO must be from Part B. Candidates are advised to make reference to their laboratory work wherever appropriate.*

PART A 1.   Classify the major types of personality theory and discuss their relative advantages and disadvantages. 2.   What do you consider to be the chief importance of studies of primitive communities for the study of personality? 3.   *Either*: what are the main criticisms that have been made of the psychoanalytic account of personality, and how far do you think they are justified? *Or:* What, in your view, is the value of the theory of the unconscious for the understanding of human personality? 4. Critically outline the theory of psychological types as used *either* by Jung *or* by Kretschmer. 5. Discuss *one* theory of personality that has emerged as a result of factor analysis.

PART B 6. How would you design an experiment to determine the relative effectiveness of massed and distributed practice in learning? Give details, indicating what factors you would expect to influence your results and how you would control them in your experimental design. 7. Show what is meant by (a) the *validity* and (b) the *reliability* of a psychological test, and indicate how such properties may be assessed. 8. Outline one method of measuring experimentally people's attitudes to different races and nationalities. Indicate the value and limitations of the results thus obtained.

C. FINAL PSYCHOLOGY EXAMINATION FOR THE GENERAL DEGREE OF BA, 1954

PAPER I (Three hours) *FIVE questions to be answered.*
1. Critically examine two theories of colour vision in the light of the known facts of colour sensation. 2. "There is a range of distance over which the perceived size of an object remains approximately constant." Discuss. 3. "We must distinguish habit from the utilisation of habit." Discuss. 4. Give a brief account of the psycho-physiology of disorders of language. 5. Distinguish carefully between a sentiment, an attitude and a personality trait. 6. Are the factors extracted from a table of intercorrelation coefficients best considered as being identical with human traits or simply as "principles of classification"? 7. Critically examine Lewin's notion that some tension system is always necessary for activity. 8. "The type theory of personality merely signifies a failure in the attempt to measure precisely the extent and intensity of personality variables." Discuss. 9. "Social psychology *is* the study of social attitudes." Discuss. 10. Critically examine the part played by maturation in human development. 11. Distinguish between the reliability and validity of a mental test and state briefly what methods have been used to assess these two characteristics. 12. Discuss the general psychological causes of aggressiveness in children.
PAPER II (Three hours) *FIVE questions to be answered.*
1. To what extent are factors of temperament influential in the determination of character? 2. "Insight is not an *explanation* of learning but a *description* of what happens when a problem is solved." Discuss. 3. What means did Freud employ to solve the problem

presented by the wide divergence in expression of human instinct? 4. Explain the meaning of the term "levels of significance" in sampling statistics. 5. Discuss some of the problems involved in the definition and verification of human abilities. 6. Compare the behaviouristic and conative theories of personality. 7. State and discuss the means by which functional integration is achieved in the human nervous system. 8. Write a short essay on the general nature of thinking. 9. "Prejudice in social life is a reflection of group influence rather than of personal experience." Discuss. 10. "The Intelligence Quotient is constant throughout life." Discuss. 11. Write an account of the chief stages in the personality development of the pre-school child. 12. Examine the contention that many social psychological processes are unconscious both in origin and in mode of action.

PAPER III (Three hours) *Write essays on TWO of the following topics.*

1. Methods of assessing qualities of personality. 2. Psychological theories of association. 3. The nervous impulse. 4. Social interaction. 5. Stylistic descriptions of personality. 6. Variations in the general level of intelligence. 7. Home versus school influence in child development. 8. Psychological motives.

PAPER IV (Six hours) *TWO tasks to be attempted.*

1. Design and execute an experiment to demonstrate the phenomenon of "spread of effect". Not more than four subjects need be used. 2. Using the method of paired comparisons and an appropriate rank correlation formula, estimate the degree of agreement between your subject's preferences and your own for the given material. Obtain also measures of consistency for your subject and yourself. 3. Apply small sample statistical methods to ascertain the extent to which the horizontal-vertical illusion constitutes a statistically significant quantity. N is not greater than 30. 4. Ascertain whether a difference exists in the size of errors made when drawing freehand horizontal lines equal to standards of 5 cm. and 1.5 cm. respectively. If there is a difference, is it statistically significant? $N1 = N2$, not less than 100. 5. Analyse the following table of test intercorrelations as far as the first residual matrix. *[A table of positive correlations between four tests was presented here.]*

D. FINAL PSYCHOLOGY EXAMINATION FOR THE GENERAL DEGREE OF BA, 1959

PAPER I (Three hours) *Answer FOUR questions. Candidates are advised to make reference to their laboratory work wherever possible.*
1. What is meant by the term "habituation"? Outline the main characteristics of habituation and illustrate this part of your answer with experimental data. 2. Is learning possible without rewards? Discuss this question in the light of your knowledge of one latent learning experiment. 3. Write a critical account of the rationale underlying the use of standardised psychological tests. 4. Examine the application of Hull's Two-Factor theory of inhibition to exploratory behaviour. 5. Examine the relevance of Lloyd Morgan's Canon of Parsimony to experimental studies of animal behaviour. 6. How far can behaviour be usefully explained by reference to a number of innate drives? 7. "Every sentiment tends to include in its system all those emotions which are of service to its ends, and to exclude all those which are useless or antagonistic." (SHAND.) Discuss. 8. Critically discuss some of the basically different approaches to theory construction in contemporary psychology. 9. Describe *one* animal study of experimentally induced conflict and discuss its application to the understanding of human neurosis. 10. Write brief notes on *three* of the following: (a) the drive-reduction hypothesis; (b) overlearning; (c) supernormal sign-stimuli; (d) external inhibition (Pavlovian); (e) the distinction between a reflex and an instinctive pattern of behaviour.

PAPER II (Three hours) *Answer FOUR questions, TWO from Part A and TWO from Part B.*
PART A 1. Critically evaluate the changes incorporated in Thorndike's later learning theory. 2. What is the "hypothetico-deductive method"? Illustrate and discuss in relation to Hull's *Principles of Behaviour*. 3. What are the major sources of difference between the learning theories of Tolman and Hull? 4. Write a critical account of the main principles in Skinner's theory of behaviour. 5. Examine the evidence on the basis of which Hebb postulates a difference between early and late learning, showing how far you consider the distinction to be a useful one.
PART B 6. Examine the relevance of the concept of "sentiment" to *social* psychology. 7. In the light of subsequent research evaluate Freud's view of the qualities of the successful leader. 8. Discuss some of the principal psychological aspects of propaganda. 9. Examine one attempt to apply factor analysis to social psychology. 10. Discuss the

influence of social norms upon cognition.

PAPER III (Three hours) *From Part A answer TWO questions, and write an essay on ONE of the subjects from Part B.*

PART A 1. "Psychology arose historically out of a mass of different traditions." (PETERS). Illustrate and give instances of this statement. 2. Assess the influence on psychology of Descartes' dualism. 3. What are the defects in the view that all our actions are "really" selfish? Discuss in the light of your knowledge of the history of psychology. 4. What was the theory of the association of ideas? Trace its development from Hobbes to Brown and James Mill. 5. Outline and evaluate Herbartian psychology.

PART B 6. The uses of introspective method in psychology. 7. The psychology of clothes. 8. The psychophysical methods. 9. Psychology and Ethology.

PAPER IV (Three hours) *Answer FOUR questions, TWO from Part A and TWO from Part B.*

PART A 1. Evaluate the "Rivers" theory of dreams. 2. To what extent is it true to say that the main phenomena of abnormal psychology can be produced hypnotically? 3. "Every schizophrenic is hallucinated some of the time and some schizophrenics are hallucinated all the time". Discuss. 4. Explain what is meant by "nemesism" and discuss the usefulness of this concept for the understanding of abnormal behaviour. 5. Evaluate the application of Gestalt psychology to the understanding of paranoia.

PART B 6. In a public opinion survey on capital punishment, two of the questions asked were: *Question 1.* Do you think capital punishment should be retained? *Question 2.* Do you think people who are mentally ill should be locked up? The answers to the questions are given below. Do people who favour capital punishment also favour the view that people who are mentally ill should be locked up? Briefly discuss the psychological implications of the result. *[Frequencies of agreement and disagreement to each pair of questions were presented here. $N = 1,000$]* 7. (i) Write brief notes on the following tests stating the reasons for their use: (a) t-test; (b) F ratio test; (c) chi-square test. (ii) A group of eight Arts students solved a problem in a mean time of 30 sec. The sum of squared deviations from zero was 800. A further group of eight Science students solved the same problem in a mean time of 25 sec. The sum of squared deviations from zero was 600. Are the two groups drawn from the same population? 8. A group of students were ranked in order of their ability to do practical work in psychology. Their examination marks for theoretical psychology are given with their rank score in the table below. What do you conclude from this table? *[A list of examination marks was presented here for 11 students, with each one's rank in a practical task.]* 9. A group of 3,600 urban children have a mean of 100 and a standard deviation of 12 on an intelligence test. Determine: (a) The 1 per cent confidence limits for the mean. (b) The standard score of an urban schoolboy who scores 118 on the test. (c) Whether a group of 2,000 rural schoolchildren, who have a mean of 99.7 and standard deviation of 10, can be said to have been drawn from the same population as the urban schoolchildren. 10. Design an experiment to determine the effects of various amounts of alcohol on a simple tracking task. State the assumptions you have to make in using the statistical method you choose and briefly indicate the steps in the calculation of the results.

E. FINAL EXAMINATION FOR THE HONOURS DEGREE OF BA IN PSYCHOLOGY, 1959

PAPER I (Three hours) *Answer FOUR questions.*
1. Is the doctrine of instincts dead? Discuss with reference to recent research. 2. How far do factor-analytic theories of intelligence conform to the ordinarily accepted criteria of a scientific theory? 3. "The choice for psychology is between working with easily verified but largely trivial or irrelevant propositions and working with complex propositions in the field of common experience, which are fully empirical as any but much harder to verify" (LAFITTE). Discuss. 4. How important a place would you give to the concept of "inhibition" in psychology? 5. Evaluate the usefulness of the concept of "introversion-extraversion" in psychology. 6. "The most important part of an honours psychology course is the training in statistics and experimental design." Discuss, indicating reasons for your agreement or disagreement. 7. Discuss constancy phenomena in perception with particular reference to their place in psychological theory. 8. "The science of those occurrences which, by their very nature, can only be observed by one person" (BERTRAND RUSSELL). Does this statement still apply to any parts of modern psychology? 9. Examine the validity of the criticism of psychoanalysis that it places too little emphasis upon certain aspects of the mother-child relationship.
PAPER II (Three hours) *Answer FOUR questions, TWO from Part A and Two from Part B.*
PART A 1. "Common-sense explanations of actions usually take the form of assigning an objective or classifying them as instances of traits

or habits. They also postulate efficient causes where these are external stimuli which set off a train of behaviour." (PETERS). Elucidate this statement with reference to the kind of function you expect explanations of behaviour in *scientific* psychology to perform. 2. "Hull's work is more valuable as a paradigm of method than as an addition to the body of psychological fact." (BORING). Discuss. 3. What do you understand by the term "operational definition"? Discuss the uses and limitations of such definitions in psychological theorising. 4. "The system set up . . . confines itself to description rather than explanation. . . . As to hypotheses, the system does not require them." (SKINNER). Do the details of Skinner's theory seem to you to justify these remarks? 5. Elucidate the logic of the use of formal systems in scientific theorising with particular reference to the work of Lewin.

PART B 6. Evaluate some attempt which has been made to interpret perception in terms of Pavlovian conditioning. 7. Evaluate the contribution of the Ethologists to the understanding of perception. 8. "If a comprehensive scientific theory of perception can be constructed then the philosophical puzzles about perception . . . will, as it were, wither away." Indicate reasons for your agreement or disagreement. 9. Evaluate applications of Hullian theory to perception. 10. "We interpret the events around us in accordance with our accumulated past experience and present needs." (HUNTER). Illustrate and discuss.

PAPER III (Three hours) *Answer FOUR questions.*

1. Discuss the "J-curve" hypothesis. 2. "Man is the most emotional of all animals." (HEBB). Examine this statement in the context of social psychology. 3. Give an account of any two methods of constructing attitude scales and discuss their relative advantages and disadvantages. 4. "A considerable measure of co-operativeness and sensitivity to the feeling and opinions of the group must be combined with independence to make the really successful group leader." (THOULESS). Discuss. 5. Discuss the contribution of psychoanalysis to social psychology. 6. "Aggression is always a consequence of frustration." Discuss. 7. "Animal systems of communication possess in rudimentary form most of the basic characteristics of human language." Indicate reasons for your agreement or disagreement. 8. Discuss the use of documentary sources in social research. 9. "Social psychology is not a science; it is only the hope of a science." Discuss.

PAPER IV (Three hours) *Answer FOUR questions.*

1. Discuss the contribution of depth psychology to the understanding of emotional development. 2. "There are no two individual birds of any given species which, when living together, do not know which of the

two has precedence and which is subordinate." Discuss. 3. Evaluate Piaget's contribution to the developmental psychology of thinking. 4. "The animal which can deal so wonderfully effectively with a normal situation may be helpless if the situation is altered even slightly from the normal." (THOULESS). Discuss in relation to arthropod behaviour. 5. "It often looks as if the trainer were pulling or pushing the animal to the desired spot by invisible wires." (HEDIGER). Discuss in the light of your knowledge of animal psychology. 6. "The need for social interaction is evidently one of the most powerful motivating forces among chimpanzees." (NISSEN). Discuss. 7. Discuss the importance of the problem of individual differences in the context of developmental psychology. 8. Discuss the phenomenon of "defence by colour". 9. Examine the principal advantages of the study of human psychological processes from the standpoint of their development.

PAPER V (Three hours) *Answer FOUR questions.*

1. "The history of psychological *experiments* is profitable, but the history of psychological speculation, divorced from experiments, can be weary, stale and flat." (PRATT). Discuss. 2. How would you assess the effect of Plato on subsequent thinking about psychological matters? 3. Outline the general approach of the scholastic philosophers to psychological issues, with especial reference to the work of Thomas Aquinas. 4. Outline the approach to mental illness to be found in the *Malleus Maleficarum* and assess its importance and subsequent influence. 5. "In the first place, I put for (*sic*) a general inclination of all mankind, a perpetual and restless striving of power after power, that ceaseth only in death." Discuss Hobbes' theory of motivation in the light of modern psychology. 6. Was Locke's *Essay* mostly psychology or mostly epistemology? 7. "On the whole, Kant delayed rather than furthered the progress of psychology." (PILLSBURY). Discuss. 8. "Here is a kind of *attraction* which in the mental world will be found to have as extraordinary effects as in the natural, and to show itself in as many and various forms." (HUME). Discuss eighteenth- and early nineteenth-century associationism in the light of his statement. 9. What was "classical introspectionism"? Trace the history of its decline and fall.

PAPER VI (Three hours) *Answer FOUR questions.*

1. Discuss the relative advantages and disadvantages to psychology of theorising in physiological terms. 2. "The properties of individual neurons and of many neurons in combination with each other are basically the properties of the nervous system." (MORGAN). Illustrate and discuss this dictum. 3. In the light of the evidence evaluate the

popular view that alcohol is a psychological stimulant. 4. Give an account of the structure and functions of the autonomic nervous system, showing how its action is related to any *one* important type of psychological phenomenon. 5. Discuss theories of cutaneous sensitivity. 6. Outline the theory of colour vision which, in your view, accounts most satisfactorily for the phenomena such a theory is required to explain. 7. Give an account of the principal motor systems. 8. "Were there no sense of smell there would be no gourmets, only consumers of nutriments." (GELDARD). Discuss, indicating the more important phenomena of olfaction and what is known of the nervous mechanisms mediating them. 9. Indicate the principal functions of the gonadal and gonadotrophic hormones, and discuss the extent to which they may be used to explain human, adult sexual behaviour.

PAPER VII (Three hours) *Candidates should attempt ALL Section A, TWO questions from Section B and TWO from Section C. They are advised to spend approximately equal amounts of time on each section.*

SECTION A 1. (a) In a sample of nine people the variance on a test (S-squared) is 4. What is the sum of the squares ? (b) Two boys of the same age are given two different intelligence tests. The results are as follows: *[The boys' individual scores were presented here, with group means and standard deviations.]* Which boy's score is the better? (c) Give one good reason why the arithmetic mean is preferable to the mode as a measure of central tendency. (d) Sketch some approximate curves of the chi-square distribution. (e) For testing significance concerning the product-moment correlation when would you normally use the (i) t test; (ii) Fisher z transformation? (f) Why do we use t tests? (g) What is the F distribution used for? (h) What is the chi-square test mainly used for? (i) The formula for a linear regression line can be written as y = a + bx. What does b represent? (j) The product moment correlation may be written as *[The formula was presented here]*, and the correlation ratio may be written in the analogous form *[Formula given here]*. What do S-squared and S'-squared denote? (k) Assuming a relationship exists, which value would you expect to be larger, the product moment correlation or the correlation ratio? (l) Define the Type I and Type II errors. (m) As Type I error increases, what happens to Type II error? (n) Test A is the most powerful test of its kind. For a sample of 80 items in test A another test B requires 100 items to attain the same power. What is the power efficiency of B? (o) When using the analysis of variance for one criterion of classification: (i) what is the null hypothesis you are testing, (ii) which statistic do you use to test the null hypothesis, and (iii) what assumption do you make? (p) In analysis of variance with a single criterion of classification one obtains an estimate of the population variance based on the sum of squares between groups and another estimate based on sum of squares within groups. Why is F calculated by dividing the former estimate by the latter? (q) What are the hypotheses you are testing when using analysis of variance for two criteria of classification? (r) Give two assumptions that underlie analysis of variance when two criteria of classification with one item per cell are used.

SECTION B 2. What do you understand by the following terms? Give examples to illustrate each term where this is appropriate. (a) A sampling distribution. (b) The standard error of a statistic. (c) A parameter. (d) A random sample, simple sample, stratified sample and cluster sample. (e) The null hypothesis. 3. Give *four* measures of association and discuss the conditions under which you would use them. 4. Sixteen students, matched for intelligence and age, were given a simple tracking task to perform and their error scores were recorded. The students were trained on a tracking task similar to that on which they were tested, and then retested, a record being made of their error score. The table of error scores before and after training are given below. What do you conclude from this experiment and what assumptions have you made in the statistical test you have used? *[A table of scores for each student before and after training was presented here.]* 5. In a study on the communication of technical information it was found that senior managers and departmental managers scored as given in the table shown below. Both groups were subjected to the same test of technical information. The information was known to have been given to the firm. It was also known that technical information was not normally distributed in either group. Analyse the data and comment briefly on the results. *[A table of five scores for senior managers and nine scores for department managers was presented here.]* 6. In a study on the physiological aspects of skill, an investigator suggested that manipulative skill was related to the general size of the individual. A group of candidates was graded according to skill at a number of manipulative tasks and then split into two groups according to size – large or small. The results are given in the table below. Analyse the data. What are your conclusions? Comment on the experiment. *[A table of scores for Good, Average and Poor performers who were either Tall or Small was presented here.]*

SECTION C 7. If the regression line of two variables was curvilinear, what statistics would you use to measure the degree of correlation?

Give any comments you think relevant on the use of this statistic. (a) If the value of the statistic = 0.5 for a sample of 131, with 11 categories of classification, is the value significant? (b) The product moment correlation for the same data is 0.4. From this result would you be prepared to say that the regression line was not linear? 8. "A statistical hypothesis derived from the data may be expected to fit the data, more or less; but the statistical calculations are intended to show how well or badly it does fit . ." (W. E. HICK). Discuss this statement with special reference to Type I and Type II errors. 9. Twenty-five students were taught the same part of the syllabus by five different lecturers. Five students were taught by each lecturer and they were allocated to the lecturers in a random manner. At the end of the lectures all the students were given a standard test on the part of the syllabus taught. The results are given below. Comment on the results and give your opinion on the design of the experiment. *[Scores were presented here for each of five students allocated to five different lecturers.]* 10. In a study of the effects of benzedrine on problem solving behaviour a Latin square design was used. Since a certain amount of practice effect was anticipated in solving the problems, which were of equal difficulty, the columns of the square refer to the order of attempting the problems, the rows refer to the individuals tested and the letters refer to increasing doses of benzedrine. Below are given items necessary for the analysis. Complete the analysis and interpret the results. *[Five relevant equations were presented here.]* 11. What distinctive contribution do you think statistical decision theory makes to the analysis of psychological data? Illustrate your answer by reference to empirical studies.

PAPER VIII (Three hours) *Answer FOUR questions.*

1. Examine the psychological aspects of one of the neuroses. 2. In the light of your knowledge of psychosis and mass media, design an investigation into the effects of the introduction of television into a mental hospital ward. 3. Examine the principal differences between hallucinations and percepts. 4. Critically evaluate the "stimulus theory" of the dream. 5. Examine schizophrenic thinking. 6. Evaluate the usefulness of Menninger's concept of "repudiation of masculinity". 7. "We ourselves, in fact, can experience in dreams almost all the phenomena to be met with in insane asylums." (WUNDT). Discuss. 8. Examine the hypothesis that "true paranoia" is basically different from, and not a sub-category of, schizophrenia. 9. "The nature of an individual's unconscious motives is revealed by the effect of his actions and behaviour upon others." (REIK). Discuss.

PAPER IX (Three hours) *Answer FOUR questions.*

1. Examine predictability of behaviour in the criminal recidivist. 2. Describe some experimental investigation of groups in industry, other than the Hawthorne study, and comment on the findings. 3. Examine the view that the concept of the "accomplishment quotient" has misled teachers and educational administrators. 4. If you were asked to study the communication of technical information in an industry, how would you do so? 5. *Either:* Discuss the grounds and implications of the British Psychological Society's recommendation concerning Secondary School Selection "that procedures should be planned and supervised by persons with adequate psychological and statistical training." *Or:* "Public distaste of the 'eleven plus' has led to a whole crop of schemes designed to do away with it altogether or at least to remove some of its worst features." Discuss. 6. Taking *one* psychiatric case that you have seen, discuss it in terms of the tests or other techniques you would use to assist the psychiatrist in his diagnosis. 7. Discuss the psychological aspects of technological change. 8. "Some people write as though everybody is either a visile or ought to be." (PEAR). Examine this statement in the context of the teacher-learner relationship.

APPENDIX 3: SOME EXAMINATION PAPERS FROM THE 1960s

A. Intermediate BA, 1964 (Four subjects were studied in year one for this examination, reduced to three in 1965-1966.)
B. First University Examination for BA or BSc, 1969 (Three subjects were studied in year one for this examination.)
C. Single Subject Honours BA Psychology, 1964
D. Single Subject Honours BA and BSc Psychology, 1969

A. INTERMEDIATE PSYCHOLOGY EXAMINATION FOR THE DEGREE OF BA, 1964

PAPER I (Three hours) *Answer FOUR questions, THREE from Part A, and Question 8 from Part B.*
PART A 1. Assess the contributions of B. F. Skinner. 2. Can you reconcile Bartlett's findings on remembering with those obtained from experiments on nonsense syllables? 3. Discuss the influence of set upon perception. 4. Discuss the concept of insight in relation to studies of animal behaviour. 5. Explain and discuss the principal differences between percepts and mental images. 6. "The basic experimental procedure is that we hold all stimuli constant except one, and this one we manipulate or vary as our demands dictate." (UNDERWOOD). Discuss this dictum in the light of your knowledge of experimental psychology. 7. Write an essay on the study by psychologists of human intelligence and ability.
PART B 8. Write brief comments (about ten lines) on *six* of the following: (a) fixed action patterns; (b) habituation; (c) the savings method; (d) learning sets; (e) haptic after-effects; (f) immediate memory; (g) the validity and reliability of psychological tests; (h) the psychophysical methods.
PAPER II (Three hours) *(Answer FOUR questions, THREE from Part A, and Question 8 from Part B.)*
PART A 1. "Personality theories are frequently packaged in a great mass of vivid word images which may serve very well as a means of persuading the reluctant reader but which frequently serve to cloak and conceal the specific assumptions which underlie the theory." (HALL and LINDZEY). Discuss. 2. Consider the relative worth to the psychology of personality of the concepts of 'type' and 'trait'. 3. "Of all the theories of human behaviour, psychoanalytic theory is by far the

139

most comprehensive and insightful account of the dynamics and development of personality." (SARNOFF). Do you agree? 4. Discuss the relative importance of heredity and environment in the determination of behaviour. 5. To what extent has the study of mental illnesses increased our understanding of normal human personality? 6. "Our civilisation is not only a right-handed but a masculine one." (ADLER). Discuss. 7. Evaluate Eysenck's approach to the study of personality.

PART B 8. A recent experiment on problem solving used problems matched for difficulty. Under two different conditions subjects matched for ability reached the following numbers of correct solutions. *[Values for ten people in two conditions were listed here.]* (a) Calculate whether there is a statistically significant difference between the two mean scores; and (b) explain the rationale underlying the procedure you adopted. N.B. For $df = 18$, $t = 2.101$ at $p < .05$, and $t = 2.878$ at $p < .01$.

B. FIRST UNIVERSITY PSYCHOLOGY EXAMINATION FOR THE DEGREES OF BA AND BSc, 1969

PAPER I (Three hours) *Answer Question 1 and THREE further questions.*

1. Write brief comments on *all* of the following: (i) the moon illusion; (ii) absolute thresholds; (iii) proactive inhibition; (iv) eidetic imagery; (v) nerve cells; (vi) receptors; (vii) anticipation method; (viii) habituation. 2. What methods can be used to give an illusion of depth on a cinema or television screen? 3. "Nor can we expect to understand the essential correlates of perceiving by adhering to those conceptions of the nervous system which view it as a passive receiver of sensory information" (TEUBER). Discuss. 4. What changes occur in remembered material as a result of its social transmission? Illustrate your answer by reference to experimental findings. 5. Examine the implications of experiments on short-term memory. 6. How is the strength of a stimulus represented in the brain? 7. Write a short essay on the components of the brain. 8. What are the main features of an instinctive response? 9. What problems was Ebbinghaus attempting to solve? How successful was he? How far have we improved on his methods?

PAPER II (Three hours) *Answer Question 1 and Question 2 and TWO further questions.*

1. Write brief comments on *all* of the following: (i) normative

reference groups; (ii) social deprivation; (iii) phenotype; (iv) critical period; (v) test norms; (vi) mental age; vii) mental subnormality; (viii) projection. 2. In an attempt to develop a simple measure of fatigue, six drivers were studied in a discrimination task before and after an unbroken drive of 120 miles. The number of errors they made is listed below. *[Values for six people before and after driving were presented here.]* (a) Do the data indicate any statistically significant change over the period in question? (b) Criticise the design of the experiment and suggest improvements. (c) What is a sampling distribution and how is it related to a raw scores distribution? Use the data given above to illustrate your answer. (d) What are z scores? Demonstrate their usefulness by considering the case of another driver who, during a repetition of the experiment, made 11 errors in the task before the drive. (Assume $\sigma = 3.0$ for this task). 3. Discuss psychology's contribution to the understanding of racial prejudice. 4. What are the main factors involved in person perception? 5. Write a brief essay on the effects of early experience. 6. Examine the methods which have been used to study the genetic basis of behaviour. 7. "We have rejected the psychiatric framework outright, preferring not to be bound and constrained by diagnostic schemes of dubious validity and unknown reliability" (Eysenck). Discuss. 8. Discuss the significance of work on the relationship between personality and physique.

C. FINAL EXAMINATION FOR THE HONOURS DEGREE OF BA IN PSYCHOLOGY, 1964

PAPER I (Three hours) *Answer THREE questions.*
1. Describe the physiological basis of any one motivational system. 2. Indicate the importance of the work of Sperry. 3. What is the difference, physiologically, between being asleep and being awake? 4. What is known of the physiology of speech and language? 5. Write a short essay on binocular vision. 6. What kind of experimental evidence would convince you that a function was "localised" in a particular part of the brain? 7. What are the implications of Land's demonstrations for theories of colour vision? 8. Describe and assess current theories of cutaneous sensation. 9. Consider whether Gestalt psychology contributed to our understanding of brain mechanisms.
PAPER II (Three hours) *Answer THREE questions.*
1. "The child is father to the man". Discuss in terms of *either* human *or* infra-human organisms. 2. Compare the structure and function in different species of the sense organs of any one sensory modality. 3.

Do humans have instincts? 4. "Man is not simply a very clever ape, but a possessor of mental abilities which occur in other animals only in the most rudimentary forms, if at all". (DOBZHANSKY). Discuss. 5. By what means may the changes in behaviour due to environment become innate in the species? Give examples from laboratory studies and from the study of species in the wild. 6. Discuss the development of thinking in children with particular reference to the work of Piaget. 7. What do we know about the mechanisms involved in the migration of animals? 8. "Precise comparative behavioural studies of fishes, amphibia, reptiles and birds do *not* support any notions that these forms differ significantly from each other or from mammals with regard to the complexity of the total behavioural repertoire displayed." (PRIBRAM). Discuss with particular reference to animal learning. 9. Examine the problems of measuring the effects of ageing upon performance.

PAPER III (Three hours) *Answer THREE questions.*
1. Consider the efficiency of remembering. 2. Assess the significance of experiments which reveal one-trial learning. 3. Discuss the learning and forgetting of skills. 4. Assess the importance of vigilance studies. 5. Why should human subjects be influenced by events that might have happened? 6. As a psychologist, what suggestions would you wish to put forward towards reducing road accidents? 7. Consider the problem of shape discrimination. 8. Discuss different kinds of perception of movement. 9. Why do thresholds vary?

PAPER IV (Three hours) *Answer THREE questions.*
1. "Between behaviour in the laboratory and behaviour in the world there is no sharp break." (HOMANS). Evaluate this statement with reference to studies of conforming behaviour. 2. Discuss problems involved in the measurement of attitudes. 3. Consider the value of cognitive dissonance as an explanatory concept in social psychology. 4. "We see things not as they are but as we are." (PATRICK). Discuss the implications of this statement for an understanding of person perception. 5. To what extent is the development of social psychology handicapped by an inability to measure intragroup interaction? 6. Examine the role of the first-line supervisor in industry. 7. Evaluate attempts to understand the structure of primitive societies in terms of psycho-analytic concepts. 8. How far can an organization be defined adequately in terms of a series of communication channels? 9. Discuss the relationship between job satisfaction and behaviour.

PAPER V (Three hours) *Answer THREE questions.*
1. Discuss the psychology of compulsive-obsessional behaviour. 2. Examine the value of the concept of mechanism of ego defence for the

understanding of personality. 3. Evaluate attempts which have been made to understand personality through systematic examination of individual differences between perceivers. 4. Discuss mania as a form of psychosis. 5. "The sensory stimuli that reach us during sleep may very well become sources of dreams." (FREUD). Discuss. 6. Evaluate Bleuler's view that the schizophrenic is characterised by "a disorder of association and by a splitting of the basic functions of the personality." 7. "Intelligence is X% hereditary". Are statements of this sort appropriate? 8. Describe some of the cognitive deficits often associated with damage to the parietal areas in man. 9. Brain tumours are often described as focal lesions; what sorts of physiological disturbance can they produce in other parts of the brain?

PAPER VI (Three hours) *Answer Question 1 (Section A), ONE question from Section B, and ONE question from Section C.*

SECTION A 1. Answer briefly the following questions. (i) Under what circumstances might a correlation of zero fail to indicate absence of systematic relationship between two sets of data? (ii) A long term study in a laboratory rat colony yielded a significant product-moment correlation of +.73 between maze learning ability of parent rats and their offspring. A regression equation was fitted to the data to enable prediction to be made from parent ability to offspring ability. It was found that predicted standard scores for the offspring tended to cluster near to the mean of the distribution. Where parent standard scores were high, predicted standard scores for offspring were somewhat lower and vice versa. Would it be valid to conclude that biological regression is operating? Give reasons. (iii) Give simple examples of a situation in which probabilities can be added and a situation in which they can be multiplied. (iv) In a vigilance experiment with male and female subjects it was found that the standard deviation of performance scores for the male group was lower than that for the female group. How would you test for the possible significance of this difference? (v) The following are hypothetical scores on tests in mental arithmetic (equated for difficulty) under four degrees of sleep deprivation for six subjects. *[Values for six people in four conditions were presented here.]* (a) What technique would you use to analyse these data? (b) What steps would you take to facilitate the computations involved? (You are not required to perform the calculations.) (vi) What are confidence limits?

SECTION B 2. In a shape discrimination experiment animals were required to select one from a display of five shapes. After training, eight animals out of twenty tested chose the correct shape. The results were set out as follows: *[Expected and observed numbers of successes and failures were presented here.]* A two-by-two <u>chi</u> square was calculated: [((16 x 8) -- (4 x 12)) squared x 40] divided by [20 x 20 x 28 x 12] = 1.9. (a) Discuss the errors involved in the use of two-by-two <u>chi</u>-square in this situation. (b) Suggest valid statistical methods which might be used for assessing whether the number of observed successes is significantly different from chance. 3. Design an experiment to investigate the effects of different amounts of alcohol upon performance in a tracking task. Discuss the form of analysis you would use in evaluating the results. 4. A group of 300 schoolchildren are given an English essay test and given marks ranging from 0 to 10 on the quality of their performance. After three months of classes in grammar they are given a further essay test and again marked from 0 to 10. Discuss *three* possible ways in which the effects of the intervening teaching in grammar might be assessed. Which way would you regard as best? (Give reasons.)

SECTION C 5. "Psychologists have come to depend more and more on non-parametric statistics for the analysis of their experimental results, but 'normal' theory provides a more thorough conceptual model than any other." (R. S. RODGERS). Comment. 6. Discuss, with examples, the rationale underlying statistical inference. 7. Examine and criticise *either* the use of factor analysis in the field of intelligence testing *or* the use of mathematical models in psychology.

PAPER VII (Three hours) *Answer THREE questions.*

1. "Although Aristotle made little empirical contribution to psychology, he made a considerable *conceptual* contribution, which included a demonstration of why mechanical types of explanation will *never* be of much use in psychology." (PETERS). Discuss. 2. Examine the approach of the scholastic philosophers to psychological issues. 3. Trace the rise and fall of the demonological conception of mental illness. 4. Evaluate Berkeley's contribution to the understanding of visual perception. 5. "Since the time of Hobbes and Locke, England has been the country which has done the most for psychology." (RIBOT). Examine the view that it has not been possible to agree with this statement at any time since 1880. 6. Consider the uses made of the concept of 'inhibition' in psychological theorising. 7. "The intellectual splendour of mathematics and physics has bewitched scientists working in the early development of other fields." (SMYTHIES). Discuss the extent to which this statement is true of psychology. 8. Examine the distinction made by Deutsch between 'generalisatory' and 'structural' types of explanation in psychology. 9. "The experiments and theories of Pavlov, Hull, Tolman and the other

great figures of learning theory have an immediate connection with the molar aspects of human behaviour usually dealt with by psychiatrists and students of personality." (EYSENCK). Discuss.

PAPER VIII (Three hours) *Write ONE essay from the following subjects.*

1. Informal leadership. 2. Attention. 3. Genetics and behaviour. 4. The physiology of learning. 6. Alcohol. 6. Intelligence. 7. Emotion. 8. Extinction.

D. FINAL EXAMINATION FOR THE SINGLE SUBJECT DEGREES OF BA AND BSc IN PSYCHOLOGY, 1969

PAPER I (Three hours) *Answer THREE questions.*

1. "There is no systematic, overall theory of hearing" (LICKLIDER). Where are the main deficiencies and the most satisfactory areas of auditory theory? 2. Discuss the physiological basis of any one biological drive. 3. Do the prefrontal areas of the brain perform the same function in man as in other animals? 4. Discuss, in terms of physiological psychology, the limits of human performance for one situation in the everyday world. 5. Write a short essay on the physical basis of memory. 6. Compare and contrast ways, both physiological and psychological, of measuring emotion. 7. Discuss how colour is represented in the brain. 8. Comment on the differences between the theories of (a) Lashley, (b) Hebb, and (c) Miller, Galanter and Pribram on the organization of the brain. 9. How can work on the properties of single nerve cells help our understanding of the behaviour of the whole organism? 10. What roles have been proposed for the lateral interaction mechanisms found in sensory systems?

PAPER II (Three hours) *Answer THREE questions.*

1. Discuss the principal variables in mother-infant interaction. 2. "Child psychology is a field of science without a natural history." Discuss. 3. Examine the evidence indicating that biological rhythms are partially controlled by oscillators within the organism. 4. Write an essay on social signalling systems in animals. 5. Consider critically the use made of the concept of maturation in studying behavioural development. 6. Discuss the importance of reafference and its relationship to the development of visually guided behaviour. 7. "Language is not only a means of generalisation; it is at the same time the source of thought" (LURIA). Consider this statement in relation to studies of early cognitive development. 8. What implications do studies on the behaviour of sub-human primates have for our

understanding of human behaviour? 9. "The process of discrimination is fundamental to the development of behaviour." Discuss. 10. How may genetical techniques be used to analyse the physiological substrates of behaviour? 11. "There is early adaptation but is there early learning?" Comment in the light of research on the newborn. 12. Examine the uses of psychological techniques in the training of subnormal and handicapped children.

PAPER III (Three hours) *Answer THREE questions.*

1. Examine in detail some approaches to the study of accidents. 2. Discuss, with reference to one area of research, how far we have advanced our knowledge of verbal learning in the last decade. 3. Is aggressiveness acquired? 4. Examine the problem of retrieving information. 5. How far do skilled responses depend upon retention? 6. Can transformational grammar be said to be more than a heuristic concept? 7. Assess the significance of vigilance studies. 8. Discuss the statement that the concept of limited capacity is a convenient fiction. 9. Relate the experimental work on exploratory behaviour to teaching.

PAPER IV (Three hours) *Answer THREE questions.*

1. Consider, with examples, how personality is reflected in behaviour. 2. In what circumstances do stereotyped judgments change? 3. "It is the goodness of fit between the human work organisation and the technological requirements that ultimately determines the efficiency of the whole system" (TRIST). Discuss. 4. Examine Lowin's conclusion that "only the report by Coch and French can be said to clearly document the value of participative decision-making". 5. Evaluate recent studies of non-verbal communication in interpersonal behaviour. 6. Consider the current validity of Allport's (1935) suggestion that "attitude" is the central concept of social psychology. 7. What use is contemporary psychology to industrial operatives and managers? 8. "As much progress can be made toward formulating general laws of social behaviour by studying the complex conditions to which they apply as by creating unusual conditions to simplify the relationships" (SCOTT). Discuss. 9. Critically examine recent approaches to cognitive consistency. 10. How far do reference groups determine individual behaviour?

PAPER V (Three hours) *Answer THREE questions.*

1. Discuss the aetiology of schizophrenia. 2. Examine the relationship between personality types and psychiatric illnesses. 3. Compare the accounts of the self given by Kelly's Personal Construct Theory and any other theory of personality. 4. "Hebb's intelligence A should not be

equated with Spearman's 'g'." Discuss. 5. How far can specific cognitive deficits help to reveal the location of a focal cerebral lesion in the human? 6. Discuss the experimental evidence that imbeciles can abstract and generalise from previous learning. What implications have these findings for the management of the severely subnormal? 7. Discuss the relation between feelings of guilt and psychiatric illness. 8. Indicate the ways in which hallucinations can be experimentally produced, and evaluate the usefulness of this type of study. 9. Examine the ways in which scientific studies of normal dreaming assist us to understand *either* (a) neurosis *or* (b) psychosis.

PAPER VI (Three hours) *Answer ALL parts of Question 1 in Section A, ONE question from Section B and ONE question from Section C.*

SECTION A 1. (i) Why are parametric tests more powerful than non-parametric tests? (ii) Three men have one throw each at the bullseye on a dartsboard. A has a probability .3 of hitting it, B has a probability .5, and C has a probability of .6. What is the probability: (a) That all three will succeed? (b) That *at least one* will succeed? (iii) It was required to know whether scores on the AH5 intelligence test would be significantly affected if the test had been taken a year previously. The AH5 was administered to a group of 40 people, and they were all re-tested one year later. (a) Name *four* ways in which we might test whether scores had improved significantly. (b) Given that 30 out of the 40 showed improvement, use any one of these ways to test for significance. (iv) Is it possible to find a non-significant product-moment correlation when there is a perfect systematic relationship between two sets of data? Explain your answer. (v) Define in one or two lines each of the following: (a) The standard error of a statistic; (b) Central Limit Theorem; (c) Confidence limits; (d) Addition of Variances Theorem. (vi) Three different age groups, each consisting of ten subjects, are individually tested in a vigilance experiment for an hour on each of five successive days. (Scores obtained are number of correct detections out of a possible 20 in each hour session.) What information would the appropriate statistical analysis yield?

SECTION B 1. Criticise the investigation of the AH5 intelligence test outlined in Section A Question (iii). Design a more rigorous investigation which includes test-retest intervals of 6 months, 12 months and 18 months. 2. Discuss in detail how the relationship (if any) between personality variables and driving skills might be investigated. 3. Design an experiment to discover whether the ability of school children to learn by rote against a background of noise differs with age.

SECTION C 1. (a) Discuss and illustrate the rationale underlying the two forms of the t test for assessing the significance of a difference between means. *[Formulae for t were provided here.]* (b) What assumptions underlie the use of t, and how important are they? 2. Write an essay on the uses and abuses of chi-square. 3. Discuss and illustrate the foundations of factor analysis.

PAPER VII (Three hours) *Answer THREE questions, at least ONE from each section.*

SECTION A 1. "Although Aristotle made little empirical contribution to psychology, and though he had a limited conception of scientific method, he made a considerable *conceptual* contribution to psychology" (PETERS). Discuss. 2. Examine, in the light of more recent developments, accounts of the relationship between 'mind' and 'body' put forward during the seventeenth and eighteenth centuries. 3. Evaluate older and more modern hedonistic theories of motivation. 4. Trace the influence of physiology and neurology on the development of psychology during the nineteenth century. 5. "In the two centuries which intervened between Hobbes and Bain a succession of English and Scottish philosophers contributed a great deal to the foundations of psychology" (HEARNSHAW). Why, then, did psychology develop so slowly in this country after Bain?

SECTION B 6. "The notion of a plan that guides behaviour is quite similar to the notion of a program that guides an electronic computer" (MILLER, GALANTER and PRIBRAM). Discuss. 7. What are the important differences between contemporary mathematical theories of learning and those earlier theories of learning which used mathematics? 8. Discuss the distinction between "structural" and "generalisatory" explanations of behaviour. Illustrate this distinction by reference to Deutsch's theory and any other theory of behaviour. 9. Evaluate the arguments for and against the positivist's eschewal of theory construction and hypothesis testing. 10. State what you consider to be the lasting influence of *either* Tolman *or* Hull.

PAPER VIII (Three hours) *Write ONE essay from the following subjects.*

1. Memory disorders. 2. Walden Three. 3. Psychological tests. 4. Space travel. 5. Fact must be the bootstrap of belief. 8. Probability. 7. Authority. 8. Psychosomatic phenomena. 9. Piaget. 10. Through the looking glass. 11. Thinking.

INDEX OF NAMES